Annie's Story

Memories of life in Garndiffaith

by
Annie (Nancy) Harris-Grinnell

Dedicated to Jade 18 years and Angharad 15 years,
my lovely granddaughters.

Introduction

I started to write these stories whilst I was in the Rhondda Trust, Royal East Glam Hospital, Llantrisant, South Wales in 2002. I cannot thank the staff enough for looking after me for so many weeks that I was there. There are too many to name but I shall always remember them all. During my stay, my daughter and I became friendly with a family from Treorchy Male Voice Choir and when they knew I was writing a book they wanted to read what I had written so far. When my daughter took me outside the hospital in a wheelchair they were outside as well and they came on to me and said, *'we loved your stories, it reminded us of our experiences during the war days when we were children, we loved it and could not put it down. We hope it will be a best seller and a film.'* I was ever so pleased because they didn't know me but they loved my book.

It's not easy writing a book, but I've enjoyed every detail that I have written about. These stories are all true. I am sorry if I've left anybody out because I can only remember so much. It was a long time ago.

My book starts when I was about 10 years old in 1942. I am Annie Grinnell and I am 70 years of age this year and I have been in and out of hospital like a yo-yo! My daughter Julie is a gem and she does her very best for me besides running her own hairdressing business and rearing two lovely girls, Jade, 18 and Angharad 15 years old.

My daughter came to pick me up for the weekend to stay with them, they live 25 miles away in the Rhondda Valley. Next morning she said *'Mam are you alright?',* '*I feel awful Julie',* '*I think we had better get you in for another check up'* she said. So off we go in the ambulance. On arrival they put me in a little ward of my own until they found me a bed in the ward upstairs because I have a sickness bug and kidney infection. Apparently there is a bug going around so they put me in Room 19 all on my own. I didn't like it much because I am deaf and small spaces make me claustrophobic. When the antibiotics started to work I felt a bit better so I started to write a letter to my friend Joan, when my granddaughter walked in and wanted to read it. Afterwards she said, *'I have never had a letter Nan, will you write me one'.* I said *'I'll do better than that, I'll write you a book.'* So here goes!

Evacuees from London

Mam had a letter from London from my brother Trevor Harris who was in the Army. He said he was getting married to Inza Gronow a Londoner from Hendon. None of us could go up to the wedding, because it was too dangerous. They were being bombed day and night by the DOODLE BUGS! that the Germans were sending over. They didn't have a pilot, it was a new invention of the Germans and they were causing a terrible lot of destruction in London. The engine in the DOODLE BOMB would only reach so far into England, so we were very lucky they didn't come to Wales.

Mam wrote back to Trevor and wished them all the best and crying at the same time. Fancy I'll have someone in London as part of the Harris family. London sounds like a big place to live, my brother Trevor has to go to the Desert to fight the Germans, he'll be called a 'Desert Rat', Mam is so proud of him, even our Headmaster, Sid Griffiths writes to him and tells him what is going on in the village.

Peggy Gronow's wedding with Inza as bridesmaid.

I think the War is going to last a long time. The Germans are bombing the big cities all over the country. There is going to be a meeting in the Garn Hall tonight, they are going to bring some of the children from London to us to stay until the War is over. Mam said we can take a few in. Our Trevor's wife had a big family, she had two brothers in the army fighting the Germans, they were George and Albert, her other brothers were not old enough to fight, they were called Allan and Peter and she had a younger sister called Brenda, so Mam and Dad decided to let them all come and stay with us.

The day came when we went to meet them off the train down at Victoria Village Railway Station. We were all excited as we saw the smoke from the train in the distance. There were loads of children on the train, it was full of evacuees and they all looked the same with their names pinned to their coats and their boxes strapped to their shoulders with their gas masks in. We had to carry them about with us all the time in case the Germans attacked us and tried to gas us!

The Gronow family had arrived, I'll never forget Brenda's hair, it was bright red and they all spoke with a posh cockney accent, we had a job to understand them and they had a job to understand us. Later on their mother came down to stay so Mam and the neighbours Lil and Rees Morgan took some in, they had one son of their own Reesy but we were one big happy family in those days, we would share everything.

Garndiffaith billiard players with a trophy during the 1930s. Front row, first on the left is my brother Will who owned the local fish and chip shop for many years.

They all started to go to school with us, so did the other evacuees in the village. It was strange having these funny speaking kids in the school. One day our headmaster, Mr. Sid Griffiths had us all in assembly and he said 'NOW CHILDREN' I want you all to welcome these children from London, don't they speak nice, you will all have to take notice and learn from them how to speak properly.

My father Joe and my brother Harold worked down Viponds colliery. They didn't have anywhere to wash in the pit, and they used to come home as black as soot, so Mam would boil lots of water in saucepans and she had this massive black kettle with a brass handle and the fire would be half way up the chimney and the water would be steaming hot ready for them to bath in front of the fire in this long tin bath. Our fireplace was huge and Mam used to cook rabbit stew in a big pot hanging on a hook over the fire. She would put any bones she got from the butcher in to give it a bit of flavour and we used to eat it all, but I cannot eat rabbit any more. Enough was enough!

Our Dad loved fish, so when Mam was lucky to get one, she would clean it and cook it in front of the open fire, she had a fork with a long handle and when the herring was cooking it smelt wonderful. She would keep turning it over until it was lovely and brown. I never saw anybody eat as slow as my Dad, he wouldn't disturb a bone on that fish, all that was left would be the skeleton. He always gave me some of his dinner off his plate and it was lovely. Dad always swallowed it down with a flagon of rough cider. I can smell those herrings now.

Mam's Medicine Cabinet

Mam was Nurse, Doctor and Midwife, whenever any of the neighbours were ill they all came to her. You only had to cough and out came the Goose Grease and a piece of my Dad's flannel shirt and if you had a fever, down would come the dried Elderflower that would be hanging up on a hook in the back kitchen and with that she would make a hot drink, it smelt vile but we would hold our nose and down it would go, sometimes she put it in a bowl of boiling water and put a towel over our heads to smell the fumes, she would say 'kill or cure' anyway I'm still here to tell the tale.

We didn't have a posh surgery in those days, it was a little hut with an old oil lamp that used to smell terrible and gas lighting on the wall. People used to wait outside in the cold because of the fumes. But we had some lovely doctors. Dr. Verity was getting very old and he would send Mr. Teague his manservant up Cwmbulla Mountain opposite our village to collect spring water from the stream. It was freezing cold but it was lovely to drink. He was about 85 years old and he had a

The top of High Street, Garndiffaith in about 1918 when it housed the Post Office with the Mason's Arms public house next door.

lovely white beard and was very distinguished looking. A new doctor came and he was called Dr. Wilson and nobody used to go to Dr. Verity after that, so he retired.

Dr. Verity used to visit his patients in a horse drawn trap and it was kept in a shed next to the surgery but unfortunately it got burned down.

When it was Mam's birthday I would go up the woods and pick bluebells and some wild daisies for her. That bluebell field was something special to me, it smelt wonderful and will stay in my mind forever.

When they bloom in summer I always think of my mother. My mother's brother was the black sheep of the family, but I loved him best of all. He was the youngest brother and his name was Cordy Clarke. He never had a care in the world and there wasn't a day that you would see him sober. He was always drunk.

Uncle Cordy and two pals sat outside the Hanbury Hotel during the 1940s.

He also had a dog and he would call around the family every day and we would give him clothes to wear but you would never see them on him because he would sell them to buy cider. He was a kind, sweet man and he would always listen to your troubles and always had plenty of time for you. All my cousins loved him. He used to make us laugh and if you asked him what size shoes he wore, he would say, 'ANYTHING FROM A SIZE 6 TO SIZE 11'. He used to make us laugh so much and he would walk in my mother's house with a big bunch of daffodils for her, most probably he'd picked them out of somebody's garden and you would know he wanted something. But the Harris's, the Clarkes, the Thomas's we all loved him dearly.

There was always a lot of singing in the house, Dad played the piano and anything he heard once he could play it by ear. Vera Lynn was always on the wireless singing to the troops that were in the Forces. I'll never forget that song 'We'll Meet Again', it was so sad. Every Sunday after dinner my aunties and uncles, my sister and some cousins would all come around and we would have a lovely time around our Dad's piano, then in the night we would play cards for money, only pennies that's all, because it was illegal and if we got caught by the 'bobby' you would get the summons.

You didn't need an alarm clock to get up in those days when it was lambing season, they would wake you up, BA!, BA!, BA! crying for their mams. They would come down off the mountain into everybody's garden and make a terrible mess. People would try anything to keep them out but they were very clever sheep and they knew their way around, sometimes the baby lamb would get lost and it wouldn't stop crying until it found its mother. You couldn't get any sleep, it was terrible early in the morning. The older sheep taught the lambs every trick of the trade so they would know their way around the following year. I have seen grown people cry over the mess these animals have made. Also they would tip all the ash bins over looking for scraps of food. If anyone came here from away they were amazed to see sheep roaming the streets, they thought it was funny, but we didn't.

Street Games

We used to make up our own games. We would play games on the neighbours by stuffing paper up their drain pipes and lighting it with a match. It would make a terrible roaring noise. Our Post Mistress had a little window on the side of her house and we would knock it and run away. Kick the can was one of my favourites. It was an empty tin

Mam, Dad and myself at home when I was 18.

and you would kick it and run away and hide but one day Ira Jones caught the can in his shoes and it landed on his head. He had to have stitches in it. My brother Harold would try and make a kite for me but it was ever so difficult because we only had newspaper to make it with and they wouldn't last long but off we would go up the Garndiffaith fields where there were always plenty of other kids trying to get their kites up as well. It was great when you succeeded. We would play in the fields all day.

Della and I would go up the Welfare Grounds to play on the swings and after we would watch the old men playing with these heavy black balls on the grass, it was called Bowls. We thought it was terribly boring but they seemed to love the game. We were not allowed to play tennis we were too young, anyway neither of us had a tennis bat.

When it was bonfire night, Dad and my brother Harold would make me a real lantern out of a jam jar and an empty tin which they would knock holes in, put in a candle and make a handle out of a piece of string and when it was dark we would carry it in our hand and it would glow in the darkness and you would see other kids in the distance with theirs. We had to be careful because of the blackout. We had some fun with those. We also played 'top and whip 'which was a small piece of wood with a nail in the bottom for the 'top' and a piece of string tied to a long piece of wood for the 'whip'. We would colour the 'top' in pretty colour chalks and then make it spin by hitting it with the 'whip' and it looked like a magic rainbow.

We all had a bath on Saturday night, out would come the carbolic soap. I hated the smell of it, sometimes it was red but when it was white you could see bits of dirt in it where Mam would have scrubbed the floor with it.

How poor can you get and know no difference to the loveable surroundings I had

Snow was coming, Mam said she could smell snow and she was always right. We all loved it when it snowed because the Clarkes and the Watkins families would try and beat each other to see who could make the best sleigh. My sleigh was broken so my cousin, Ray Clarke, and I decided to go and look for some wood to make a new one. He said, we'll go up the Undertakers after school but don't tell the other kids, its got to be a secret. Mr. Griff Williams was the Undertaker and Elvet Rawlings was his apprentice years later. Griff was a distinguished looking man with a long moustache and he would put wax on it and it stuck out from his face. He looked so elegant when he walked in front of the funeral in his black top hat and the family would walk behind the coffin in those days. He kept the horses in the stables in front of the school. We asked him for wood to make a sleigh because my sleigh wasn't any good any more and he said *'Come back tomorrow I'll see what I can do for you'*. Next day we couldn't get out of school quick enough, the snowflakes were falling like half-crowns. Won't be long before High Street will be covered. Mr. Williams gave us some lovely long bits of wood and we made the best sleigh of all the other kids.

When it snowed really bad nobody in the village could go to work. We lived high up in the village and they would be all day shovelling a way clear to get to the shops and trying to clear the roads

A 19th century local public house which is no longer in business 'The White Horse'.

for the buses to get to Pontypool. Once they were open there would be a fleet of trucks full of snow from Pontypool Town Centre coming up the hill. They would be all day dumping the snow, anywhere they could find in Garndiffaith, back and fore. I don't remember anyone making any fuss about it, after all it was only a bit of snow, soon washed away with the rain. We don't have those snow falls like that any more. They were so much fun when you were a child. We used to make a slide in the playground of the school and we would slide from the top to the bottom, it was ever so fast and by the time the school bell rang our feet would be soaking wet, it's a wonder we didn't catch pneumonia but we didn't seem to feel the cold in those days. We were hardened to it. The slide was so fast it would bring tears to our eyes and we could have broken our necks. Some of the teachers liked to have a go they were like 'Kids at Heart'. We played hopscotch also and we would draw an aeroplane on the ground and jump in the squares, that was fun.

I joined the Girl Guides but I cannot remember much about it. I had a uniform and when the village had a big event like a Carnival we would all walk behind the Band. There was always something going on, never a dull moment. The boys had the Boys Brigade and you would wake up to the 'Thump of the Big Drum' they would wake the Devil himself.

Garndiffaith Boys Brigade.

The Angel In The Chapel

We lived next door to the Sardis Chapel which was very old and had gravestones in it. On my way to school I would pass this Lonely Big Angel, who was bigger than me and she looked so cold in that grey coloured stone, all alone in the corner of the graveyard.

I had a lovely pet rabbit but my mother used to let it run loose in our garden. One day I came home from school and I couldn't find him. I expect he went into the graveyard and I never saw him again.

When the Sardis Chapel had their Anniversary everybody could go to the tea party on the Monday. You had to pay one shilling and us kids from the other chapels would be there. You don't see that anymore. They would all walk the streets with their new clothes on. They have knocked down the Sardis Chapel and built new houses on the ground, but I think my Angel is still there in my thoughts.

Christmas had long gone and the summer was coming, I would be leaving school in October 1946, my last days at school.

Mr. Sid Griffiths our Headmaster was a very strict man, some boys stole some ponies off the mountain and ran away on them to join the Army. They were only about 12 to 13 years old. They were nowhere to be found, so they had to call the Police for help to try and find them. Eventually they were found on the banks of the canal near Abergavenny. They were on their way to Brecon. After a few days back home they all came back to school. Mr. Sid Griffiths was waiting for them. He lined them up and made them bend over and he gave them a good tanning with the cane and they never ran away again.

Every one of the children in the village had some sort of animal, but mostly they had a rabbit. One of my cousins, the Clarkes wanted one but he didn't have a hutch to put it in, so he went down the ash tip to see what he could find. It was his lucky day, when he got there they were emptying the lorry and an old sideboard came off it. My cousin said *'Can I have it'* and the lorry driver said *'Yes'*. He immediately took out the drawers and threw them on the tip because he only wanted the other part and, as he did, £1 notes which had been under the newspaper in the drawer started to fly everywhere. He picked the money up and ran off, forgetting all about the his rabbit hutch. After that all the kids used to go down the ash tip looking for buried treasure but they were never so lucky as my cousin.

There was only one man we didn't like in the village, he lived in the middle of High Street and when the snow was down he would try and stop us sleighing past his house. He would come out with red hot ashes and throw it all over the road but we would fill it all back again with snow and sleigh away. You cannot imagine that happening today. We would sleigh from the Garn Hall all the way under the Viaduct Bridge and it was thrilling, no cars about in those days.

There was a big empty house down the Rookery by the river and we all thought it was haunted. It was by Granny Walls shop so we used to go down there a lot to play. It was about four storeys high and when it was dark we used to dare one another to go inside and get to the top and you had to wave your hand out of the window. I used to be scared stiff but I remember doing it. There was another shop down there called Hilliers, you had to walk up a lot steps to go in but it was a quaint old shop.

MARK ALEXANDER was the wealthiest man in the village who had a shop on High Street and he owned a lot of houses which he rented to people. He owned nearly all the houses and our Mam used to pay him 7/6d (37½p new money) a week for rent every Friday. His daughter Lilian would come and collect it but he would never do any repairs, it was in a bad condition when it rained. It came in everywhere, down the walls, Mam had to move my bed not to get it wet, but she would never move because she loved living there. She could have had a Prefab at the time but she would not move.

Her door was always wide open and she would put the rent money, insurance money and the cheque-man's money on top of each book. They always came on a Friday because that was pay day. The cheque-man was for clothes you could buy and she used to pay a few shillings every week.

Dad was 50 years old and Mam 42 years old when I was born in 1932. There were some beautiful women born at that time in the thirties, Elizabeth Taylor, Princess Margaret and Me. I was Annie Harris, youngest of six children. Mam lost one and I had three older brothers and one sister May, who I followed everywhere, even when she was courting. I was like her shadow. Judy Garland and Liz Taylor were my idols in the films and I saw a lot of the world through their eyes. Exotic, wonderful places, I used to imagine I'll go there one day. Fancy Liz Taylor marrying a Welshman, Richard Burton, although he left his wife for her, it was very sad at the time.

Being so young with brothers old enough to be my father wasn't easy, as I got into my teens they used to watch me like a hawk. They always called me The Scrapings Up. But they were always there for me, even after I got married to Leonard Grinnell. I was in my teens and one day in school I didn't feel too well, so I ran to my sister's house, I had terrible pains in my stomach. My sister gave me a pain tablet and put me to bed. Then we had a long talk about the birds and bees and I realised I was now a woman. I was afraid to tell my mother, I thought I had done something wrong. She was so strict.

Mam did the Pools Coupon every week and she always said *'We'll be rich one day'*. Saturday evening news on the wireless and the football results, everybody had to be as quiet as a church mouse. When it finished we would say *'Any luck Mam'*, she would say *'No, but wait until next week I'll have it'*, but she never did. I remember one of my friend's sisters, Annie Motley winning the pools and they went to live in Bournemouth and we never saw them again. When Mam wanted to decorate the house you had to go to the builders yard and order the wallpaper out of a great big book with all wallpaper in it. If you wanted to write a letter to anyone you had to use pen and ink which you bought from the Post Office, Freddy Edwards was there then and his sister Dorothy and their Mam and Dad ran the shop opposite the Garn Hall. It was a busy little sweet shop but we were always out of sweet coupons.

My mother never wore any make-up in her life, she was always my Mam in her Welsh shawl around her shoulders and her hair tied up in a bun. I remember our next door neighbour who was always looking glamorous and I used to watch her when she was making herself beautiful. Her ingredients were gravy browning, a tooth brush, a match box and a tin of dark boot polish and a pencil. Her husband was Colin who was an electrician and he was a very clever man who was always mucking about with anything to do with electronics. One day Mary called us in and to our amazement, Colin had made a small television about the size of a small plate. The picture on it was wonderful. He didn't have a cabinet around it only this small bulb to look at. We didn't have a set in our house then, so we thought it was wonderful. Many years later be became a councillor and then Mayor of Pontypool. We were all very proud of his achievements. Mary's hair had a few grey hairs so she would put the boot polish on with a tooth brush and she would strike matches and rub it on her eye brows and lashes. She would draw a line up the back of her leg with a pencil and put gravy browning on her legs to make people think she had stockings on. She always looked lovely. I cannot bare to think what happened in the rain.

Annie (left) and her sister May in 1960.

When Mam and Dad had the pub in High Street the village was very busy. There were always lots of people doing their shopping and I was born in the pub The Butchers Arms. Mam used to buy all the barrels from Mr. Stedman on Talywain. My brother was a little devil, one day he went down the cellar and got a hammer and hit the stopper off one of the barrels and it exploded and he flooded the cellar. I was only a baby then. We had a well in that cellar, so Mam had to lock it up after that. My grandad Clarke had the Stones Pub, Victoria Village many years before, it was a quaint old stone public house and the trains used to be at the top of the garden, you could smell the engine smoke as it passed by.

When grandad died, my uncle Jim Clarke who was in the 1914-18 war took it over. He was wounded and lost an ear in that war and when his wife died they named me after her 'ANNIE'. I always hated that name so everybody called me 'NANCY'.

A few doors away lived my other grandad Harris on Stoney Road. It was a big white house and he had a big garden full of roses, right up to the top of his garden onto the railway track. My Dad would take me down every Sunday. Grandad would give me an apple and we were never allowed to run about. We had to sit quiet all the time we were there until it was time to go home. When he died and I got married my mother gave me a Staffordshire Blacksmith that belonged to him. I still have it, it's very special to me.

Sunday School Trip to Seaside

Once a year we went to Barry Island, Mam would cut all the sandwiches and make sure we had plenty of drink. On the way before we arrived near Barry Island we would look out of the bus and see in the distance the sea in front of us. What excitement there was on that bus. When we arrived we would make our way down to the seafront where there were these long rows of wooden tables and seats where we would all sit and have our sandwiches and they would sell us big pots of tea and then opposite was the Ice Cream Parlour

Myself, my elder brother Will and Mam sat in front.

where you could buy a bucket and spade for a few pennies. We all loved that trip to Barry Island. To finish the day we all went into the sea and ended up on the beach making sand castles and watching Punch and Judy and playing ball. What a grand day it was for all of us, young and old, we used to say *'Roll on next year'*.

Pit Explosion

We came out of school one day and something was wrong, everybody was out in the street. I said *'What's the matter?'* to one of the neighbours and she replied *'There has been an accident down the Vipond Pit and some of the colliers have been buried in coal'*. Oh! My Dad and my brother Harold are down there and I couldn't find my Mam, she had gone up to Viponds Pit to wait with the other women for survivors, so I went to look for her. The only way they could get out of the pit was up the Bond Cage Lift and one by one they were coming up. Luckily Dad was OK but my brother Harold was buried alive, but they got him out in time, his legs were hurt so they brought him home in a wheel barrow. Mam had to bath him outside in a long tin bath. Dad had a lovely long grey moustache and a beautiful head of curly grey hair and when he came home from the explosion it was all as black as soot. We were all happy to see them alive. He later went to work at Blaensychan Pit.

The mountain was all lit up that night, the miners with their head lamps lit and the mountain was a glow from the steel works in Ebbw Vale, which was the other side of the mountain. In the evening when they opened their furnaces, it would light up the whole of the sky like a rainbow, only much brighter. It was all gold and red in colour. Dad and Harold went back to Viponds and stayed there. My father retired at 70 years of age and they gave him £5 and a certificate. That is all he had!

My brother Harold and Mam in the 1940s.

The Prize Fighter Boxer - Pete Stephens

There was a very tough, short man who lived down Davis Court, Garndiffaith. He was a fighter and used to win prizes. One of his children had to be corrected in school and the Headmaster gave him the cane. Next we knew Pete Stephens was up the school and hit Sid Griffiths down the school steps. I don't know who I was most scared of, the School Master Sid Griffiths or the boxer, Pete Stephens. He gave up boxing later because he was punch drunk Sid Griffiths wasn't afraid of anyone, but if he saw Pete Stephens coming, he'd be gone like a shot.

Boys and girls and teachers at the Garn School with Annie in the front row, second from the left.

Last Few Days at School

Myra Griffin was in a higher class than me, but we seemed to get on well together. One day she was going to Roberts the Hairdressers in Pontypool to have her hair done. She said she didn't have to pay because apprentice girls were practising on her hair. Why don't you come with me. So off I went to have my very first hairdo, but I said *'Don't tell my Mam'*. When I came home my mother didn't recognise me. *'You get straight back down there and tell them to put it back the same as it was'*. *'Too late Mam I've had a perm'*. School next day, Mr. Griffiths, Headmaster had Myra and me in front of the class, I thought he was going to cane us, but instead he said *'Don't these young ladies look nice to go out into the world'*. We were chuffed!

Della's House

Before leaving school I used to play with Della in the field behind her house, it belonged to the Workingmens Club. One day we saw a bird going back and fore to a nest in Della's house roof, so we decided to check it out. Her Dad didn't have a ladder so we got some big nails and a hammer. I was passing the nails and Della was knocking them in when I got too close to the hammer and it went straight into my cheek and I was bleeding so Della's Mam stopped it. I never had stitches but I still have the scar on my face. I always think of that bird's nest when I feel my face. The Workingmens Club is still there, but the fields have long gone. Building Council houses everywhere. Ground was cheap then.

My best friend Della at the front of the photograph in 1946 when we were both 14.

Annie aged 14, a glamour photo taken at Osborne Studios Pontypool without Mam's knowledge!

Della's Homemade Toffee

We used to wait for Della's mother to go out so that we could make some home made toffee with a tin of treacle and I remember we had to put some vinegar in it to make it set and we would boil it up and when it was ready we put in on a tray. It always tasted a bit burnt, but we ate it although it used to make our teeth stick together. You couldn't open your mouth until you sucked it all away. I can still taste it, but we had some fun with that homemade toffee.

Leaving School

I couldn't read when I was in school and they thought I was dull, so I never went to the Grammar School in Abersychan. I was dyslexic but they didn't know too much about it in those days. Most of the people in the class passed their exams in those days. Della, Betty and I stayed in the Garn School. Our teacher was Miss Gwyneth Watkins and we would read a chapter every week out of the book Little Women. Oh how I loved that story. Rosie Shortman was a friend as well and her uncle lived in a caravan at the bottom of the Lasgarn Wood. I used to love going to see her uncle Ulic. He only had one leg and we would go up into the Lasgarn Wood, for it was safe in those days, but there is too much crime about now. The wood is still there and in the Autumn when the leaves are turning colour it is beautiful.

Della and I had a secret hiding place, it was over the river by the cricket field and it had a fresh water stream where we built our own play house out of stone from the mountain. The river water was freezing because it was coming out of the mountain. It was that clean you could drink it and you could see your face in it. Once we built it up and we would paddle in it. We used to have lovely summer days years ago. We spent many a day over the other side of the river. They were days I shall never forget.

Sister Veronica - The Nun

East Glam Hospital - June 2002

Sister Veronica was here today going around the wards visiting the patients. She read a chapter of my book and she liked it. It made her laugh, especially the bit about my mother who would keep the local newspaper and anybody's face she didn't like she would take it to the toilet with her. I wonder WHAT FOR! During her visit my daughter and granddaughter, Angharad walked in. What a surprise to see Sister Veronica because about 14 years ago, my daughter Julie lived in Cardiff and Sister Veronica who was a District Nurse to young mothers with new babies was working the area and that was where she met Julie with her new baby. She was always collecting for some good cause or another. She is a very kind and thoughtful person and she told our Julie that she had just come home from a visit to Rome. She said she had a wonderful time. Also she said to my daughter, *'I wish all the patients were like your mother'*.

The Man from Treorchy Male Voice Choir

The first week I was in hospital in Ward 19, I met a lovely family. When they rushed me in again the second time I was surprised to see that he was back in as well. My daughter was talking to him and told him I was writing a book, he said *'Can I have a look at it'*.

He and his family read it all through and to my delight they enjoyed reading it and they said it brought back a lot of memories from the past for them as well. The one sister kissed me and said I couldn't put it down, it is so good. I am really chuffed about it.

The people knew nothing about me so it's nice to have an outside opinion. I only wanted to write something for my lovely granddaughters Jade and Angharad to remember me by.

The nurses have inspired me to go on writing my book, they have been reading little bits when they had a minute to spare.

One of the nurses who is 66 years old, 3 years younger than me said, *'I remember when the Americans were here, one of the American Motorbikes knocked down her friend's sister and she had to spend one year in Llynypia Hospital and was left with one leg shorter than the other. She was given a lump sum of £6,000 which was an awful lot of money in those days.*

Two American doctors used to go to her home and give her exercises. For years she received loads of parcels from America, for which they were very grateful because we were still on rations'.

I would like to thank Nurse Jean Dousette for this wonderful story as Jean has been nursing 35 years in hospitals. She retired last week but still doing Bank Shifts.

Thank you once again, Jean Dousette.

Jean was one of 14 children, they had big families in those days but she remembers it well. She said they didn't have any evacuees because they didn't have any room for them to stay.

The River

Miss Gwyneth Watkins our school teacher was living on the other side of the river, she lived with her Mam and Dad who were getting old. She asked me would I go after school to do their shopping and any running about for them that they wanted. Miss Watkins had a sister who was also a teacher and she lived down New Inn about 4 miles away. I wasn't very old at the time, but I used to go and take things down to her house for her. I had to catch two buses to get to New Inn and it was a big experience for me to do that on my own. From then on I started to grow up. They were lovely people who I shall always remember.

Another lady who was always kind to us children lived on our side of the river, the name we called her was Auntie Jesse Rees, and you knew when anybody had fallen in the coal dusty, dirty river because she would wash and dry their clothes before their mother knew. You would see dresses and knickers all across the Cinder Row on open washing lines where Auntie Jesse lived. She had boys in the Army who went to war. People helped one and another in those days, nothing was too much trouble, it was a lovely time to live in, but frightening and you knew everybody by their first name, even their dogs.

On Mondays Mam would get the rubbing board out and that big piece of carbolic soap and sometimes it made her fingers bleed. My Dad would wash the heavy Welsh blankets in a big tub with a funny looking stick which he would beat out the dirt with. He used to wear my mother's rubber pinny not to get his trousers wet. They would be all day doing it.

View of the Cinder Row as it looked during the 1940s.

Free Shoes for Everyone in School

'Line up' the teacher said and to everyone's surprise she was measuring everyone's feet. We didn't know what was happening. Eventually the headmaster came around and told us. The Government was issuing free shoes for all school children. When they arrived we were all waiting patiently to see what we were going to get. We only had one pair of shoes to wear at that time. What a surprise when the boxes were opened to see these wooden clogs. They looked to weird and heavy to walk in but we all got used to them. You could hear the children clipperty clopping along all over the school, but you couldn't skip in them so we used to pretend to dance. I think we invented the Clog Dance. I shall never forget those clogs!

Moving to a bigger class, all the clever kids had left the Garn school to go to Abersychan Grammar, so we had to learn other things to help the War Effort. Mr. Griffiths made a garden for the boys to grow vegetables and us girls learned to knit gloves and balaclavas for the soldiers to wear on their hands and heads. It was better than the other lessons and both the boys and girls enjoyed what they were doing.

I remember 'PATHÉ NEWS' when we went to the pictures and saw the soldiers fighting, they had our hats on. I was so pleased.

Only once did anybody steal from someone. The butcher Tom Powell came up the school in quite a rage, someone had stolen his takings that were in a tin in the butchers shop. After a lot of enquiries the tin was found. One of his delivery boys who worked for him after school had stolen the money and he hid it under the gulley. He knocked a hole in the wall to put the money in and put the bricks back. He thought no-one would ever find his 'Pot of Gold', but they did. After that no-one ever trusted that boy again. He was always in trouble.

Scabies on our Bodies

Things were quite bad regarding getting any fruit to eat. If we saw the Ffyfes Banana lorry coming up the village, we would all follow it until it stopped and they would let us have one banana each.

The local nurse would come to check on us children very often, but when she came once we all had sores with great big scabs on. The children who were the worst had to go into hospital. Mine were not too bad and I didn't have to go. I remember crying because I wanted to go into hospital with my friends. They all recovered eventually.

Time to go to the Toilet

Someone's hand would shoot up in the middle of a lesson. *'Yes what is it?'* teacher would say. *'Please Miss can I go to the toilet'* and off they would go, but when they came back sometimes they would be covered in snow and ringing wet. Our toilets were at the bottom of the school yard, OUTSIDE. They were just wooden planks and they were not very nice and they were horrible, smelly things.

Home Comforts

Our toilet at home was at the top of the garden, which was shared with the neighbours next door. You had to wait if you saw a bucket of water outside because someone would be in there.

My father (Joe) sitting proudly in his garden.

Our Mam would always make a posh toilet roll. She would cut up the local newspapers into squares for us to wipe ourselves but if there was anybody's face in the local paper that she didn't like she always kept that page for herself. I wonder why? The pieces of paper were nailed to the back of the door.

Trouble with the Drains

When there was trouble with the drains we all used to go up the woods in the long grass and the bluebell fields. I bet they didn't have toilets like that in Buckingham Palace.

German Plane crashes on our Mountain

I was only little and every man in all the villages around had to join the Home Guard. When the plane crashed it didn't kill the Germans and our men in the Home Guard had to capture them. I don't know who was the most frightened, the Germans or our men.

Collecting Souvenirs

When it was safe everybody was up the mountain like a shot. They were after pieces of shrapnel and bits of the German plane. Whenever we heard the sound of those German planes after that we were always very frightened that it would happen again. But thank God it never did.

War Declared Over

People were never the same after the war. The women liked their independence and didn't want to give their jobs up and when their husbands came home things were not the same for them either. I was too young to understand grown-up things but as I grew older, I saw a lot of families going their different ways.

The Yanks have arrived

Mam always told us never to speak to strangers or the bogey man would have me. One day I was out playing with my friends and I could hear people shouting *'The Yanks are here'*. When I saw them in those funny shaped cars with no roof on them I ran straight home to my mother and I said *'Mam the bogie men have come and they are all 'BLACK''*. We had never seen a black man before. As time went on we used to follow those jeeps around everywhere because they would give us long strips of chewing gum and always bars of American chocolate.

The older girls in the village used to go out with them and the soldiers gave them nylon stockings and took them dancing and when I was older me and my friends would watch them through the window of the dance club. They would throw the girls over their shoulders and catch them on the other side, it was called the JITTER BUG. We loved it and tried to copy them, but we failed to do it. They were very fast dancers but thrilling to watch.

After the war some of our Welsh girls got married to them and went to live in America and they lived happy ever after.

Some left black babies behind and they were brought up to be Welsh kids just like us. I wanted one of the black babies when I grew up, they were so beautiful. I thought those black men were the kindest men in the world.

Labour Days

The local midwife was Nurse Munn and when she was very busy delivering babies she always sent for our Mam to help her. One of the neighbour's sons played rugby for Wales. He was an international player and when his wife got pregnant he brought her home to have her baby in Wales. When she went into labour they sent for Nurse Munn but she was with another pregnant lady so my Mam, Beat, delivered it. After that he took them to live in Australia where their little girl grew up and she married a rich sheik. Mam said she was a beautiful baby.

Kings and Queens

We never had anything such as beach chairs and fancy outside tables and loungers to sit in the sun. They were all ready made for us on the side of the hills, lovely grass settees and the smell when anyone was cutting the grass was wonderful. I remember one day our Ray was the boss and we were playing down the ash tip and he sent us all home to ask our mothers if we could have one potato, an onion and carrots, some peas and we all had to bring something back. When we got back our Ray had built a stone fire place and had lit a lovely red fire out of coal and bits of coke off the ash tip. We cooked it all and ate the lot, it was the most wonderful meal you have ever tasted. Mam never knew we were playing with fire. When we finished our meal our Ray said *'I'M THE KING AND WHOEVER FINDS A WHOLE PLATE OR SAUCER WILL BE THE QUEEN'*. I never ran so fast in all my life. I stole one of my mother's plates. I shall always remember being the *'QUEEN OF THE ASH TIP'*.

My Auntie Lil Clarke had a big cellar under her house. My cousin Ray who was two years older than me kept rabbits in there. He had all sorts, they were lovely. We used to help him clean them out. It was also used as an Air Raid Shelter. When the siren would blast, we would all make for Auntie Lil's cellar. There was no gas light in there, only a few candles, but we all had a lovely time during the Air Raid. Some of my cousins were very talented, one could play the mouth organ and the spoons and they had lovely voices. The Germans could hear us in Germany singing at the top of our voices. Oh how I loved for that siren to go off! I wasn't a bit frightened when I was in that cellar with all of my family around me.

Gronows are taking over

At first they all stayed with us in our house. I remember Brenda and myself at the top of the bed, Allan and Peter down the bottom. It was a bit of a squeeze so Auntie Lil and Uncle Rees Morgan took the boys in to make more room. They had a son Reesy, who would look after them while they were with them and he was like a brother to me and still is to this day. I love him dearly. Washing the clothes was the only problem. Mam would get up early on a Monday morning and she would fill buckets of water and put it on a roaring fire. When it was boiling she would put all the white clothes in to boil. She also had a big spoon on a handle to get out any soot that fell on top of the bucket from the chimney. My Dad would help her with the heavy bed clothes. We had a round tin bath and a big wooden dolly that he would sway back and fore in a circle. They would take all day on Mondays to do the washing.

Mrs. Gronow got a job in an engineering factory called Girlings. Our Mam used to keep an eye on the children for her and see them off to school. Christmas was near and Girlings was giving a Christmas Party for all the children of people that worked there. I'll never forget that party as long as I live. All the Gronows went and I was left behind. I remember crying my eyes out. My Dad worked in the pit so there weren't any Christmas parties down there. After that the Gronow's older sister came down from Hendon in London. We were all outside the house when she arrived with the big suitcase. I was by the door when she opened it. I was shocked, she had black-market goodies, it was full of tins of corned beef, salmon, sweets, chocolate and thousands of fags. Mrs. Gronow said *'have you got something for those kids outside?'* but I remember running away, I didn't have anything.

Brenda Gronow's wedding with Annie as bridesmaid to the bride's left.

We didn't have any money so I decided to show the cockney kids how to get some. First of all we went around everybody's house to see if they had any empty bottles to take back to the pubs. Reesy Morgan was in charge of the Gronow kids. He said we will all go up the mountain and pick some whimberries and sell them. So he gave us all a jar to fill and he said *'Don't eat any because I'll know because your tongue will go black'*.

Allan Gronow who was the oldest, Peter and Brenda and a couple of us other kids went as well. When we got up the mountain, they had never been up there, Allan said, *'Where are they?'* You have to look for them under the bushes on the ground. They are black and very small, but watch out for mountain snakes. When we have all filled our jars we will sell them for nine pence a pound. We were all tired out when we got home and Mam made a lovely whimberry tart with mine. All the money that we made off the bottles would pay for us to go to the Garn Hall to see the latest cowboy films.

After a while the Gronows settled in and Mam found a cottage behind us for them to live in. Years later the Gronows moved to Talywain and are still there. We only had two washing lines to share between six houses and that was my Mam's and a line by Sardis Chapel, so everybody would keep feeling the clothes to see if they were dry so that they could then put theirs out. We all lived down the gully archway at the back of High Street and there were some tough characters living by Sardis and you had to go through the gully archway to go to Sunday school. I would keep awake all Saturday night because the Rogers family would come home drunk and they would have a good fight. Next morning you would see them all together like as if nothing had happened the night before.

War Time Birthday Party

It was Joyce Evans's birthday party. Her Mam and Dad owned the Temperance Bar which sold lots of goodies. Her mother was a sister to my brother's wife so I was ever so lucky to be invited to her birthday party. We all dressed up in our Sunday best and when we saw all the goodies on the table it was mouth-watering. She never had a cake but instead there was this enormous Light House made of silver paper that lit up and at the end of the party they took the top off and it was full of presents for everyone at the party.

I cannot remember having any of my birthdays because we didn't have the money to buy a Light House or anything else, but I survived it by having some lovely school friends who never had a birthday party themselves either.

Hair Cut

Mr. Dai Gurney was the local barber. We didn't have a ladies hairdresser so if you went to him you all ended up with the same hair cut, short back and sides, always cut to last.

School Dinners

The headmaster and teachers would help feed us our school dinners and then us girls in class 4, last class before leaving school, would have to help feed the teachers and the younger children. I will always remember the chocolate pudding and custard and the stew, that was my favourite and when it was Christmas we had Xmas pudding with money in it. I saw the headmaster put a 3 pence piece in a pudding and I wondered who he would give it to. Guess! It was me! I was so pleased.

The Devil's Heap of Stones

The Devils black stone came out of Viponds Colliery, where my family worked during the war and for all of their lives. I am going to tell you a story from my school days.

Mr. Sid Griffiths our headmaster came into our classroom one day where we were having a history lesson and he said, *'What's the meaning of Garndiffaith in Welsh'*. We were all stunned, none of us knew. He replied *'A HEAP OF STONE'* and it is still there to this day. But we love it.

Mrs. Gronow does a round with Sid Griffiths

One of the Gronow kids had been naughty in school and if it was bad you had the cane. I don't know which one it was, I think it must have been Peter because he used to run after me and bite me all the time. Anyway Mrs. Gronow gave our headmaster one, she hit him. Mrs. Gronow was a tough woman to handle. She wouldn't let anybody touch her kids.

Annie leaving School in 1946 - aged 14 years

Oh! my God, leaving school tomorrow, I wish I could read, I'm good at counting and my friends, Della Watkins is a good speller and my other friend Betty Whittington is worse than both of us. Anyway the three of us together should get by somehow. Well girls we have to look for a job in the nearest factory which is down in Cwmavon. It's a plastic factory where they make plastic knickers for babies. I think they pay £1.12s.6d a week. So off we go to see what this place is like and to save money we will walk to the factory.

Well here we go *'Best of Luck'* to us all. Betty didn't come with us because she had got a job on the milk round over the British mountain, so Della and I went on our own. Off we went through the fields of Granny Watkins farm, we used to take a big risk going to work in the Plastic Factory in Cwmavon every morning because it was private property. If she saw you she would set the dogs after you. It was a long way around to get there otherwise. We were good runners though, so we always made sure the dogs never got us and always watched out for her walking her dogs. When it snowed we would slide down the Snail Creep which went right down to Cwmavon Road. They must have liked us because we both got the job and we started 8am on the following Monday. Cwmavon is a pretty village, it's right in between two mountains in a little valley of its own. We would have our tea break and sit on the bridge and watch the stream go by to join the River Severn a few miles away. On a clear day we can see the River Severn entering the sea and even see the other side, clear across to Weston-Super-Mare and even ships on the water.

Well we started to work at the Plastic Factory and a Sunday morning we would go and help Betty on the milk round. It was heavy work carrying those crates full of milk up the side of the British mountain but she loved the job. On our way home we would pick up free range eggs that the chickens would have laid on the side of the road everywhere. My mother was so pleased when I took them home because we were on Ration Books and eggs were like gold. Everything was on Ration Books, our clothes, sweets, fruit and food. It was awful sometimes when you fancied a nice juicy banana because there weren't any coupons left. If we saw a Ffyfes banana lorry we would follow it about until it stopped and we were lucky to have one each. Our ration was enough to last one month and then if you spent all your coupons you couldn't have anymore until next month's. We were always using next month's ration coupons.

Annie and a friend busy shopping in the late 1940s.

If someone in the village was getting married we would swap coupons so that the bride could have a second-hand wedding dress and a new pair of shoes, if she was lucky.

Annie (second right) with factory friends at Pontypool.

Della and I are going to the factory dance which is taking place up at Blaenavon Mostyn Hall. We are going to knit a jumper, both the same. We are so excited as we have not been to a dance before. Wonder what it's going to be like?

The only wool we could get was from Hayward's shop. It was fawn and brown. We decided to put Fair Isle on the top. My sister is a good knitter and she helped us to get it together. Well I finished mine but Della had two sleeves to do so I said I would help her but when we finished it, my sleeve was much bigger than Della's because I was a looser knitter than her but we had such a laugh anyway.

The day of the dance came and I was all day messing with my hair. I had terrible hair, it was so fine, it was like hair off a pig's bottom. Della had hair like a horse's mane. I always wished I had a good head of hair. As soon as it started to get evening time, I was ready to go! So here I go on my way to call for Della and when I got there they were all out. I banged on the door and shouted *'Della, where are you, don't let me down'*. I banged again, *'Della don't do this to me please'*. A neighbour came out and said *'they have all gone on the Blaenavon bus'*. I thought Della will meet me in the dance hall. I got on the private bus with some girls from the factory, they were older than me. I was only 14 years old. On the bus going up I felt very nervous and when we arrived I took a deep breath and hoped for the best. I followed the flow of girls and did what they did. I thought to myself I am 14 years old and I'm a woman now, I can do it. I was scared stiff on my own and when we got inside you had to walk the full length of the hall to go downstairs and check your coat in and I always remember the cloak lady saying *'Don't lose your ticket or you won't have your coat back'*.

The band was playing a lovely romantic tune as I came up the stairs. I wore my jumper and when I looked around at the other girls we all looked much the same in our Ration Coupon clothes. We all looked pretty poor.

I have just had three different dances, they were all the same to me as I cannot dance. I don't know my left foot from my right foot. I'm definitely going to learn.

Look out Annie, there is a chap coming towards you. I could see him through the corner of my eye, he was handsome with blond hair, blue eyes, my height. Hello!, he said to me. *'I'm Leonard, what is your name, I haven't seen you in here before'*. I looked him straight in the eye and told him a big fib. *'Oh! I come to all the local do's'*. I was trying to act older than I was and we danced together all night and it worked. At the end it was one of the loveliest nights of my life and I didn't miss Della one bit! Alas, the dance came to an end and Leonard asked if he could walk me to the bus. I said yes and when we got outside the moonlight was shining on his blond hair. He was different to me I had dark hair and big brown eyes and I had a perfect figure, I was thin and slim. My mother used to say to me *'Pull yourself in'* so I did but when I went to breathe again they popped back out again. My father who would be sitting in his rocking chair would just laugh. He was a lovely old man.

Len aged about 19.

Outside the dance hall everybody was waiting for the bus so Leonard pulled me into a doorway and started to kiss me. It took my breath away, I'd never been kissed like that before. I was glad when the bus came because my mother would have killed me if she had seen me. She was always warning me about HOT BLOODED MEN. I never knew what she was on about until that night. He frightened me to death.

When he stopped kissing me he said *'Can I see you tomorrow'*, I said *'Yes',* but I knew he was too mature for me, I was a bit afraid of him although I liked his kisses, they were devine. Home I went with a new experience to show for my first Big Dance.

Next morning it was Sunday so I had promised Betty to help her on the milk round. I felt so happy that day, I told Betty all about Leonard, but I said, *'I'm not going to meet him again, he's too fast for me and I don't know where he lives anyway, I won't be seeing him again'*. Betty said when we have finished the milk round we'll go home and have our tea, let's go to Pontypool Park on the Monkey Parade, as we used to call it. There were always plenty of boys down there and lots of our old school friends as well. If it rained we used to sit under the Grandstand, it used to get full and we had many a laugh under there. Sometimes it was freezing cold but we never felt the cold in those days. We would watch the boys kicking a ball around the rugby field. One of the boys I recognised, he was a bit on the fat side but I had noticed that he was a lovely dancer and they used to call him SHINGKY and I found out later that he worked with Leonard. He came across to speak to me in the Park and said *'That was you up the dance in the Mostyn Hall last night, wasn't it'*. I said *'Yes'*. He said *'Good night wasn't it'* and off he went after some Pontypool girls.

Len on the far left with his mates at a dance.

Another photo from one of the many local dances.

On the Monday I met Della to go to work. *'Where were you then Della'* I said and she said *'They had to go to her aunt's in Blaenavon for some celebration in her family'*. But I didn't trust her after that. In fact she did me a favour because I had my first experience of being on my own and it made me feel a bit more independent. I told her all about the dance and Leonard and she said she wishes she had known, it sounded better than the night she had.

Wednesday came around and there was a dance every Wednesday night in the Band Hall up the Varteg. I said *'Shall we go, we'll walk up and it's only a shilling to go in and they have a lovely band called the Vauxhall and we can watch and copy them doing the Waltz and the Tango'*. Later that day I started to get ready, out came that fawn and brown jumper. The Band Hall wasn't very big but when it filled up it was cosy and the atmosphere in there was electrifying, everybody was so happy. All of a sudden the doors opened and all the boys came in off the Blaenavon bus and who should be on it, Leonard. All hell broke loose, I had a tap on my shoulder, it was him, he said *'Why didn't you turn up for our date on Sunday, I waited for hours'*. We danced all night and at the end he said *'I'm walking you home, I'm not going to lose you again'*. He said *'my friend's mate in work saw you down Pontypool Park on Sunday afternoon, I'm not in the habit of girls letting me down'*. I thought to myself he's a big-headed devil, as well.

Next day in work a couple of girls came on to me. They saw me dancing a lot with Leonard, the tongues were wagging, I think half the factory had been out with him and they told me he was

18 and a half years of age, yes, 18 and a half. My mother is definitely going to kill me. I have brothers older than him. I am the baby of our family and I am only 14 years old. If our Mam finds out there will be murder in our house. Anyway Leonard is nothing but a BIG FLIRT! AND I NEVER WANT TO SEE HIM AGAIN. BUT I DO LIKE HIM.

Weather is changing, getting colder going to work in the mornings. I told Della when it starts to snow I'm going to get another job where it is warmer to work. *'When you go, I'm coming with you'*, she said. A lot of the girls in the village worked down the Biscuit Factory in Llantarnam but it was a long way down the valley but we decided to give it a try. We travelled by bus and it took us 45 minutes every day back and fore so I was too tired to help Betty on the milk round on a Sunday morning anymore. I used to have a lie in bed.

The morning we started in Westons Biscuit Factory they lined all the new girls up and they just pointed at you and said *'You up the chocolate belt and you in the creamery and you in the tin wash and you stacking the biscuits and you two (that was Della and me) on tin lining'*. There were a lot of girls of 14 years of age on that job and when you got older they would give you a more responsible job to do.

Della's father was very strict with her and she didn't come to many dances with us. I started to work up the chocolate belt tin lining and at the weekend they would let us have a big bag of Marshmallows to take home. I was still seeing Leonard but we had to keep it quiet as I was 15 years old now. I said to him one night when we were in the pictures, *'you only want me for my marshmallows'*, he used to eat the lot.

I always gave my mother all my wages when it was pay day and every Friday she would be waiting for me to come home with the money. I was coming up the path and I could see a funny look on my mother's face. I stopped dead, and my mother said *'IS THAT RIGHT YOU ARE COURTING, A RAT EATER FROM BLAENAVON.'* I nearly died of shock, apparently some man from there had eaten rats when the war was on. I said to my mother *'who told you then'* she said *'Joyce next door'*. She had spilled the beans, I was now officially dead. I didn't think Mam would let me go out again.

It was a good time before I saw Leonard again but I didn't tell him what my mother had said, because she made it quite clear he would never set foot in through her doors.

I loved my weekends dancing and I got very good. I started to go Ballroom dancing on a Monday night in the Palais, Pontypool but they were a load of snobs going there. Times were still hard if only we had more money, more coupons, more sweets, the people would have loved that, but I must say, they were very happy days and we seemed to get by.

Monday again. I hated a Monday, so did Mam, she would get up very early to do the washing and it would take her all day on the rubbing board, her fingers used to bleed. She used to put so much starch in my white overalls for work, I had a job to move in them. It had been raining all day so Mam wasn't best pleased, she had to dry the clothes in front of our fire. I just finished work and on my way home I thought I'm not going out tonight, I'm too tired. As I opened the door to go in Mam was hanging her big knickers on the line in front of the fire, there were wet clothes everywhere. She said there is someone here to see you and when I looked around the corner, there was Leonard, sat as large as life in my father's rocking chair. I was in a state of shock. Nobody ever sat on Dad's chair. I couldn't speak as the shock set in. My mother was making a fuss of Leonard and she took to him straight away. I was thinking I hope she doesn't take him in the front room, it was full of bottles brewing. Mam loved making home made wine. I would go out and pick all the Elderberry and Dandelion leaves. She would make wine out of anything, but it used to stink the house out, but some smelt lovely.

Len and Nancy following their engagement in 1951.

I looked at Leonard and said *'What are you doing here?'*. He said *'I have some bad news, I have had my Call-up Papers and I have to go into the Army'*. I started to cry because I didn't think I could take any more shocks in one day. My mother liked Leonard very much and he would always be there waiting for me to come home from work until the day came and off he went to join the REME (The Royal Electrical and Mechanical Engineers). He looked fantastic in his uniform.

When we were kids we would stay outside our Mam's window and watch the wine brewing, the bubbles going up and down the bottles and they would make all froth on the top,

Len and myself on the left with a group of friends.

like ice cream, only it was a brown colour. It was fascinating to watch and we would stay there for hours. Sometimes the bottles would go POP! BANG! And the froth would go all over the place. Mam had them all on trays and they would be full.

Our Harold, my youngest brother left school when he was 14 years old and sent to work in Blaensychan Colliery with all his cousins. They all worked together with a lot of older men. He was always coming home and making us laugh at what they used to tell him.

My auntie Lil Clarke had 24 children, but they didn't all live. She still had a big family though and to feed them all she would send them out to catch rabbits up the mountain.

There was always a big pot of stew on her fire and any other children that were there at the time she would also give some to. We had rabbit stew for dinner-tea-supper. I never want to see rabbit again. If any of the children in the village got lost they would look in at Auntie Lil's first because all the kids loved her. She was a wonderful person and when she used to laugh, her belly would shake because she was so fat from having so many children.

Big Pit Colliery Blaenavon

Leonard's dad, Jack Grinnell, was a coal cutter in Big Pit and one day one of his mates had a bad accident and caught his arm in the machine. They took him to hospital but they couldn't save his arm. He had to have it amputated. The Pit Manager wasn't very happy about paying compensation so Leonard's dad went to court to fight the case.

He won and they had to pay him a lot of money, he was very grateful.

Courting Days 1949

Len and I used to do our courting in the freezing cold outside our house just around the back. You weren't allowed to take boys home then. There was some open ground at the back of our house where people hung their washing out. One night it was dark and one of our neighbours came up the narrow path at the back of our house to get the washing in and I said to Leonard *'Be quiet we don't want to frighten her'*. Anyway, she got all her washing in her basket and started to come back down the path and I coughed. She dropped the washing and ran as fast as she could. Her husband came out and we apologised for giving her such a scare. Another night when it was raining we would go under the Gully Archway by the Sardis Chapel. It was lit up from the gas light off the road. Mr. Edmonds lived by there in the little cottages on the side. He worked in Viponds Pit and when he was coming off afternoons he would deliberately bang into us. He knew we were there and one night when I got home my mother was mad because my coat was all black from the coal dust off Mr. Edmonds dirty clothes. The next day I went and told Mrs. Edmonds what he had done and after that he always came through the Gully Archway sideways not to brush against us.

Len's father at Barry Island 'a quiet gentleman'.

Len's Demob from the Army

Leonard was coming to the end of his 18 months in the Army and what a shock we had when the Government said the boys had to do another 6 months service. We were not very happy about it, but we lived through it. It was just 2 years wasted out of our lives. But it made us both stronger in our love. I think they should do National Service today, year 2002. When he came out we got married in 1953. Things were still tough but we both worked very hard and eventually after four and a half years I became a mother and had Julie Anne.

Julie's Great Grandad's Unlucky Dustbin

We always went on a Sunday afternoon to visit Julie's great grandfather. He was 90 years of age. It was late evening and the nights were drawing in, getting quite dark and as Leonard was driving up the side road to get to his house we felt a bump on the car. We had run over great-grandad's bin and there was a big dent in the middle. We never said anything to him but the next week when we got there, great grandad said *'somebody last week ran over my dust bin and made a bloody big dent in it'*. We all looked away and didn't say a word. But I'm sure he thought it was us. We went up one day and caught him up on the ladder on the roof and his house was very high and once he knocked a hole in his bedroom wall and put all his money inside and papered it over. You didn't know what he was going to do next.

Village Carnival and Fancy Dress - 1967

My daughter Julie wanted to be Queen of Hearts so I went to town and bought yards of lovely material to make her the outfit. It took me over a week as it wasn't easy to make. The day of the carnival arrived and I was getting Julie ready and in walks the little girl from our local hotel, she was dressed as a majorette in red. She looked lovely, and then here comes Helen. *'Auntie Nancy will you dress me up, I haven't got anything to wear'*. So I went into my wardrobe and found a gypsy skirt and a white blouse and all the beads I could find and I made a big pair of earrings. She looked lovely and afterwards I put some make-up on her face. Two minutes after that my nephew came in *'auntie Nancy I've got nothing to wear'*, so I went into my husband's shed, found an overall and his REME hat that he had when he was in the army. Then I found a long brush and a pallet that you use for cementing and I stuck some coloured paint on it and with a brush I put a moustache on our Lyn's face and made him into an artist.

Off they went. What a surprise at the judging, our Lyn had 1st prize, Helen came 2nd and my daughter didn't come in it at all. So it goes to show what you can do to make something out of nothing if you try. Julie did have 1st prize with her doll and pram. We also dressed our dog, a Pekinese in clothes and a bonnet on her head, she looked ever so cute. The dog used to love

A Garndiffaith Youth Team during the 1960s.

dressing up and taking part in anything that was going on. She lived until she was 11 years old and we missed her terribly for years.

The snow came down deep over night and when we got up in the morning you could see all the neighbours shovelling a pathway to their houses. My husband was a drummer up at our local Rugby Club and that night there was a special do on in the Club House. He never left his drums in the club, he always brought them home. I said to him *'you won't be playing tonight, there's no way you can get the car out'*. The roads were all blocked and the buses had stopped running. At about 6 o'clock there was a knock on the door and to my surprise it was the Rugby team boys, they had come down to carry his drums up to the club. You should have seen the trail, one behind the other. I wish I had taken a photograph.

The club was on top of the mountain where we lived and some of the drums were quite heavy. Weather never bothered the rugby boys and the club was full that night. Someone shouted *'It's snowing again'* and they all said *'who cares we'll all sleep in the club'*.

One day they were playing a match and the secretary of the club asked me would I give a hand behind the bar as they were short-staffed. I said *'Yes'*. After the game was over and they had all showered they came rushing in for their pint. After a few they got quite merry and they started to do their Ritual Dance. Only two of them could do it though. They were fully dressed and they had to put a full pint of beer on their head and strip to the bare skin without spilling a drop of beer on them. I will never forget that day.

It's years since that happened and Dave Stevens, one of those boys, is now a grown man with a family. He was presented with a B.E.M. for services to his country by Lord Hanbury Tennison. So these daredevils of kids you never knew what they would grow up to be. My husband Leonard played for a lot of big artistes, one was Dicky Valentine who was sadly killed at Crickhowell. Leonard had played the drums for him a few nights before he was killed, he was a lovely singer.

Wednesday Night Bingo in the Garn Hall

In the 1950s we moved to Stanley Road and we had a lot of work to do in the house and garden, so we didn't go out very often because we didn't have the money. One Wednesday evening Leonard was cutting our front lawn and I was scraping old wall paper off the walls when one of my friends called in, she said. *'Why don't you have a break and come to Bingo for an hour'*, so off I went leaving Leonard to see to things. That day I had ordered the cheapest paper in the book for my living room 3/9d (19p) a roll, that was all we could afford. We were enjoying our game of bingo when it came to playing the last house, £25. Somebody called the line and my friend said *'how many do you want for a full house'* and I said *'loads, I won't win'*. I wanted 4 numbers, anyway somebody called and we were about to leave and they said *'IT'S A BOGIE CALL'*, so we all sat back down. What a surprise I had my numbers come straight out and I won £25. A lot of people had walked past our house from Bingo and of course Leonard was still working in the garden. Before I could get home everybody was telling Leonard that I had won the last house of £25, a lot money in those days. I was so mad because I wanted to surprise him myself.

The next day I went straight over to the Co-op and I ordered the dearest paper for my ceiling and it was 17/6d (87½p)a roll and it is still up there to this day, 2002. With the money I had left over I bought a Persian Carpet, my room looked a Million Dollars thanks to my game of Bingo.

Toy Factory

When I started to work down the Toy Factory, I became very friendly with a girl from Penygarn. Her name was Jean Bingham. We started going to dances together, Leonard liked her, so he fixed a Blind Date for Jean with one of his mates Horace Hill and the four of us got on very well. Jean and Horace started courting strong and to our surprise got married well before we did. It was a pretty wedding. I still have their invitation card after all these years.

I remember one night up the Varteg Dance Hall Leonard and Horace tried to make Jean and I jealous, so we left the hall early. Jean and I could hear them running down the hill after us, so we hid in a doorway. That night Jean was sleeping at my house and when we got home and opened

Annie and friends from Pontypool toy factory.

the door of my home there was Leonard and Horace having a cup of tea and supper with my Mam and Dad. I thought the cheeky monkeys, but we all had a good laugh, Mam as well.

The day came when Leonard had to go into the Army, Mam did a lovely meal for Leonard, me, Horace and Jean and we all sat down and I burst out crying. Then Jean and my Mam started and we were in tears all night but off he went the next day to join the Forces.

The Dog Stone

A very faithful dog died and his master wanted to put him where people would remember him, so he took his dead dog up the mountain and placed a stone on his grave, that's why people say today *'I'm going for a walk up the Dogs Stone Mountain'*.

The Germans dropped bombs near there in the war when they were looking for the Ammunition Factory in the area. They also dropped bombs in Blaenavon and Pontypool. They dropped a bomb on the Wheatsheaf Pub in Pontypool.

Leonard's Encounter with the Law

Leonard was stationed in Blandford which was a long way away and there was only one telephone in our village. Miss Lockyer had retired and Ted Bath took over the Post Office and they were very friendly with our Mam and Dad, so he would let Leonard ring him in emergencies or to tell me he was coming home and Mr. Bath would come and tell us.

On one occasion he didn't have enough money for the full fare on the train so he bought a railway ticket to go as far as it would go and when he got off the train at home, the Station Master caught him. He was in his uniform at the time but it didn't make any difference, he had the summons anyway and he had to go to court to pay a fine. He now has a criminal record. Thank goodness he was transferred to Bridgend after that so it didn't cost him so much for him to come home. A few times I went down to Cardiff on the bus to meet him. We would spend a few hours together and then he would go back to Bridgend and I would come home to sulk. We were very much in love.

My Glamourous Makeover

One day I had a message from Leonard when he was stationed in Bridgend that he was coming home for a long weekend. He never saw his Mam and Dad that time because he wanted to spend every moment with me. I had to meet him off the train at Pontypool Road Station. I worked near the station in the Toy Factory so I finished work early that day. I never used any make up only a bit of lipstick so that day the girls in work did my face up so I would look nice for him. I had big brown eyes and long eye lashes and they did a good job on me. When he got off the train he stopped dead when he saw me and said *'I'm not kissing you with all that muck on your face'*. I thought I was so glamorous!

1930s

Things were changing, the old King was very ill so he sent his son the Prince of Wales down from London to meet the miners and their families. He promised them better housing, better working conditions, better everything and then he went back to London. When his father died they made him King but not for long because he was seeing an American woman called Mrs. Simpson. She was divorced at the time and he was spending lots of money on her buying diamonds and lots of jewellery for her. He went abroad and we never saw him again. His brother then became King and not long after, the War broke out.

Sweets on Ration

One of my friend's mothers never gave her children any sweets. She kept them all for herself and used to give them some currants instead. I was lucky I had my Mam and Dad's and my brothers, they all gave me their sweet rations. Wasn't I the lucky one. I've thought of it many times, fancy going all those years without a taste of sweets or chocolate. I can't imagine it, can you?

Della's Dog and the British

If you went on the bus you would have a conductress who would give you a ticket for your return fare and she would clip it on her machine which was strapped around her waist. If you lost that ticket you would have to pay again. Garndiffaith was the end of the line so the driver and conductress would have a tea break in Harris's snack bar. If Della and I wanted to go over to the British after the boys, the Marshall brothers, we would put Judy, Della's dog in one of the buses and close the door but Judy always found us!

Judy was a loveable dog, a Bull Terrier, always frothing at the mouth and waiting for Della to come home from school and never leave her side.

Della and I were proper 'tomboys'. Della didn't have a bike so she would sit on the back of mine and off we would go pedalling away over to the British. There was a circle of trees over there and we would climb up to the top and have great fun. Later they put caravans there for people to live in. It was a lovely quiet place to live, birds were all around you.

Mrs. Gronow had two older boys and they were both serving in the British Services in the Army. They were away quite a long time, years, until the war was over. Albert married a German girl and George married a Scottish lass, so between the Cockney and Welsh, the German and Scots we must have sounded a bit strange when we were all together. Now after all those years they all sound the same with a bit of Welsh in them. Their children are Welsh to the bone, all with strong Welsh accents, they have even got great grandchildren now. Some live in Cwmbran New Town. I met Albert's wife a few weeks ago, she's had another baby granddaughter born last month so they are even taking over Cwmbran as well. They are really a large family now. My Mam and Mrs. Gronow have passed away many a year ago, but I would love to think of them looking down on us and I think they would be real proud of us all.

Things were moving fast again in the village, even Mr. Randle who had the slaughterhouse was moving to Abersychan. They called it an abattoir, a posh name for killing animals. Mr. Randle always looked the type, with his long bow stick, his light overalls and long wellington boots, but most of all his long stick with a hook on the end. You could see him coming for miles.

There were only five small sweet shops we could go to, Bryn's Temperance Bar, Edwards's, outside the cinema, Protheroe's, under the Hanbury Hotel, and Deakins in the High Street which was run by his daughter Mrs. Hayward but best of all was Granny Wall's down the Rookery by the river. She would always let us kids have sweets from next month's ration coupons. We all loved that old woman.

Mr. Deakins' was a little shop in the High Street, he would also take next month's coupons and was very popular with the older boys. I used to wonder what they were up to hanging about outside. So I watched my younger brother Harold one day and he went in with a couple of lads and when they came out they went straight under the Gully Archway. After a while you would see lots of smoke coming out. They were all smoking fags, 'Woodbines' they were called and if the boys didn't have enough for a whole packet, Mr. Deakin would open it up and sell them five between them. Mrs. Hayward his daughter, would sell cottons and wools and she had a son Donald who was very frail and we didn't know at the time, he was dying of some disease. It was awfully sad when he died because he was their only child. They had nobody else only each other. Mr. Hayward was a headmaster in another village and he was one of the few who had a car, a Ford Prefect.

Class Distinction

We were all Gully Archway kids and they were 'pretty tough'. If you lived in the Avenue or on Stanley Road you were somebody! Only the Co-op Managers, like Mr. Johnson and Elvet Rawlings lived on that part of the Garn. Elvet never married but he liked the women and they all loved him, he helped a lot of people.

Gambling - Money to Burn

Just after one o'clock every day, nearly everybody would make their way across Percy Street to Harry Arthur's pub or sit on the wall outside the Hanbury Hotel, where they would sit and read the daily papers and write out their horses for the day. They didn't have much money to bet so it was only 6d doubles but what fun they used to have listening on the wireless to their horse run in the race. You could hear them shouting at the other end of the street, *'come on, come on'*.

Looking back, when I think of Ivy and her husband Tom bringing us Black Market stuff from London, I used to think London was milk and honey, but it wasn't. It was right here on our very own doorsteps.

New Piano for the White Hart Pub

Only a few people could play the piano as I remember. My Dad and Eddie Britton's father. They used to play in the White Hart on a Saturday night. It wasn't very big and people would sit on the pavement outside listening, drinking and singing. They were always happy with themselves, my dog Peg was always outside, so I always knew where my Mam and Dad were. Peg was a sheep dog. I'll never forget her.

First Christmas with Toys - A Doll with a China Face

Years were passing and I must have been about 10 years old and Christmas morning had arrived. In my stocking were the usual apple, orange and a few nuts. But to my surprise I had a doll and pram. I couldn't wait to get out of the house quick enough to push it up the High Street which was very steep, when Rosie Shortman came out and said *'can I push your pram?'* and I said *'OK'*. To my dismay she pushed it hard and sent it careering fast down the road only to turn upside down. On impact my lovely china doll's face was all in pieces. I cried all day and my brother tried to stick it together with sugar and water but it never worked. That was the last of that Christmas Day.

Swimming with Look-outs

The only swimming pool we had was over the British on the side of the mountain. It wasn't very warm in there because it didn't have any roof and the walls were old tin sheets with holes in. We had to stick paper in the holes in the tin sheets to stop the boys looking in when we were undressing, they were devils.

Once a week Miss Watkins our schoolteacher would take us over there and try to teach us to swim but she never got in the pool herself, because I don't think she could swim. She had a long stick which she used to tie around us and pull us across the water. After swimming we would play in the empty coal trucks that would take the miners up the mountain to Blaensychan Mine and we would get very dirty.

It was always closed on Sundays so we used to climb over the tin sheets to get in and we had one of the boys to look out for the Bobby. He used to catch some of us and give us a warning not to do it again. But we did.

The Templars - Strict Chapel Teaching

There was Joe Templar a teacher in the big school and his sister who was Headmistress of the Garndiffaith Junior School and without them I don't know what would have happened in Sunday School in the the Wesleyan Chapel. Miss Templar taught everyone of us a poem for the Anniversary. It was hard for me because I couldn't read. The day of the Anniversary arrived and I was shaking from top to bottom but Miss Templar never failed me. When it was time to say my recitation, I would not take my eyes off her and she would sit at the bottom of the platform with her book of poems in front of her and she would lip read to me all the way to the end. What a relief it was to say that last line.

They also had a brother who was the village cobbler and his shop was by the Hanbury Hotel in Bailey Street. He used to tap our shoes, what was left of them. He was always very busy but sometimes you would go up High Street and he, Dai Gurney and Mr. Protheroe would all be outside the shop laughing and talking.

The Templars have all gone now. A pity there wasn't a street or something named after them. I think they deserved that. Never mind I will always remember them.

Raiding sheep rouse villagers to anger

This was a headline in the South Wales Argus in April 1968 bringing to everyone's attention that a state of war had been declared between residents of Garndiffaith and flocks of straying sheep. Totally fed up with the woolly marauders continually invading and ransacking their flower and vegetable gardens over the years, the locals decided that enough was enough and that something had to be done. Led by Gwyneira Clark and Nancy Grinnell, a petition was soon organised demanding action from the authorities and more than 1,000 signatures were collected for presentation to Pontypool Council Offices and a copy for local MP Leo Abse to digest. There was even a militant faction amongst the population who advocated the capture where possible of these four-legged looters, with a view to holding them to ransom! This threat was never actually carried out but, it certainly stirred the powers that be into taking notice of their constituents after years of neglect.

Leo Abse M.P., Drewi Morgan, Mrs. Clarke and myself outside my house in Stanley Road.

Two victims of the sheep incursions are seen here with Pontypool's Member of Parliament Mr. Leo Abse and other officials who came to Stanley Road to see for themselves the damage so caused and listen to the gardeners' concerns.

The Clarke Boys

They all had lovely voices and when they were old enough they went around the pubs and clubs singing in harmony. They never got paid any money, they just sang for a couple of pints but everybody used to wait for them to walk in to entertain them with a song *'Oh Jimmy Brown he's a Clown'* and so on.

The Stute

We had a small games room next to the Cinema, the Garn Hall, called the Stute. All the men would rush there after work to get a place on the Snooker table, but there was one man that no-one could beat, he was called Jones Becca. He was good and he also played the piano for the Children's Choir.

Entertaining the pensioners at Abertillery.

Choir

I had a high voice and Margaret Fry, a girl out of the Avenue and myself, always sang a duet together. We would travel over the mountain to Abertillery to entertain some old people; over there it was always a good trip out of the village to meet others. The Choirmaster was Goff Stiff and he was very strict.

The entertainers.

Anniversary Time

We had a lot of Chapels and one Church. When it was Anniversary time I would have a new dress and pair of shoes. Mam always bought my dress from the Co-op, it was always a horrible cotton old thing, but we had to spend all our money there because they used to pay you 'divy' (dividends) on what you spent and at the end of the year they would give you some money back and Mam would always buy a new bed or something.

The Dressmaker

Mrs. Jones who lived by the Cinema was a dressmaker and her daughter Pam would come to chapel with three new dresses on for the Anniversary, one in the morning, one in the afternoon and one in the evening. I will remember those dresses forever, they were all hand-smocked in pretty colour silks. They were devine, I would have died for one. I used to brush past her just to touch them. My Mam couldn't thread a needle properly, she was hopeless at sewing.

No Burglars in those Days

Mam's door was always open and we were never afraid of anyone stealing anything. In the winter our door had its own locking device. Our Dad once had to get in through the window. When the frost came the flag stones in our house would all rise out of the ground and the door wouldn't open. So we would boil a kettle and some pans of boiling water and throw it over them. The boiling water would also kill the Black Pats. They were crawly things that were under the flag stones. Another way my brother used to kill them was by putting a saucer of beer in the middle of the room and he would put small planks of wood to go up the saucer and in the morning they would be dead drunk.

Time to build the Prefabs

There were a lot of fields in the village and the Council brought people down from London to check them and so they decided to build tin houses on them. My mother didn't like them but I thought they were grand. Some of my friends lived in them after they were built. I tried hard to persuade Mam to move. I even told her about how lovely and big the windows were and they always opened, even when the frost was about. *'I don't care if they have glass chandeliers, we are staying here'*. Mam loved our neighbours and no-one wanted to move.

Hidden Money

My Dad was a very quiet man but always very thrifty. He would give our Mam enough to live on and go through the week but we never saw a lot of money about. He used to hide it from my mother when he was in work. When we used to go upstairs the pennies used to break the oilcloth on the floor where he had hidden them underneath and we used to find some in the brass knobs on the corners of our Mam's bed. The only time he gave us any was when he was drunk. He loved his bottle of cider, it was very nice and sometimes we would pinch a drop.

Christmas Goodies

All us kids went to the pictures to see Cowboys and Indians and musical films. That was the only outside knowledge we ever had. We would get very excited at Christmas because every child had a cake and an orange on that day. We had to wait in a long line to receive our Christmas cake and they used to stamp our hands when we got it. I thought we were rich and we always shared it with it with family.

Rivals for the best bonfires between the Clarkes and the Watkins

It was a busy time for all the children, everybody was out looking for anything that they could burn. We would wait for all the shops to throw out all their empty boxes and we always prayed that it would not rain. So we always worked hard to keep everything dry. Bonfire night had arrived and we were all getting our stuff ready to build our bonfire. One of the Watkins had a granddad who lived down Abersychan and every day one of them went on the bus to take him his dinner. We were all on the road when Credwin Watkins called Jeannie in to take granddad's dinner. She didn't want to go because we were all having so much fun collecting rubbish for the bonfire. Anyway one of the other neighbour's children went with her on the bus. They were running for the bus to come back when they were hit by it, Jeannie was killed but the other little girl lived.

We never had a bonfire after that, it was nearly Jeannie's birthday and her Mam put her new watch on her in the coffin. It was awfully sad. We will never forget Jeannie. The people mourned for years, even to this day, the year 2002, the Watkins family still put in our local paper, the Free Press, a remembrance to her, they also put flowers on the Bob-a-Day Road where she was killed.

My first real china doll, but only for a lend

It must have been about 1938-39. We had a lovely woman called Mrs. Gray living at the top of our road near the Gully and she was always mending and repairing things for people and I was her fetcher and carrier. I would take things for people to fit on and see if they were OK and then I'd wait until she was ready for me to go somewhere else. Mrs. Gray had two boys and a girl and they were away working. The one boy was away in the Air Force and he looked like a film star in his uniform, she always had his photograph in front of her.

Upstairs she kept all their toys from when they were young. Her daughter had a lovely china doll and it was out of this world. Mrs. Gray would let me play with it when Dorothy her daughter wasn't home. I loved that doll, nearly as much as my dog Peg.

Unfortunately, Dorothy came home unexpectedly and caught me with her precious doll and she grabbed it off me and went straight upstairs with it. Mrs. Gray shouted at her *'Give that child that doll, you are a grown woman now Dorothy'*. But I never saw my lovely china doll again.

An elephant never forgets and many moons later when I grew up and learned to drive a car, I used to see Dorothy in the bus stop waiting in the rain and I would drive straight past her.

Rags and Bones

That's what you would hear the rag man calling as he sat on his horse and cart. Everybody would go through the house looking for odds and ends, anything for a shilling or two. We never had any rags to give him because Mam cut them into long strips and we would help her to make our new rag mat, which came out only on a Sunday when the family came to visit. I loved that rag mat, so did my dog Peg, we used to lie on it together in front of that everlasting big fire. The rag man came regularly and he also sharpened our Mam's knives.

Hymn Time

Everybody was always singing. Caroline Thomas was another of one of our Mam's neighbours and on the weekend she would clean her house from top to bottom. She would be banging her straw mats against our wall and singing hymns at the top of her voice. Mam said to her, *'why are you always singing'*. She replied *'you might as well be dead if you can't sing'*. Caroline Thomas had a son Dai, who played rugby for Pontypool. He was so good they sent him away to play International Rugby. He ended up living in Australia and he's still there now.

Pubs

There were so many pubs in our village, two in some streets. Mam and Dad had one, The Masons Arms, I think it was called. I was born in it. When I got older they moved to Percy Street around the back of High Street. Everybody got drunk on a Saturday night. I would try my best to keep awake for when they came out of the pubs they would be laughing and singing and every week the Rogers family would end up fighting. Next day you would see them with black eyes and swollen faces but it didn't make any difference, they did the same thing every week. Crazy they were!

Disablement in the family

We were very lucky in our family. I had a second cousin Joan who was born with a gammy hand so she could never go to work, so on a Sunday it was her job to go to the ice-cream bar with a big dish and get the Sunday ice-cream. Our Betty Thomas was the other, she was also a second cousin. She was born with a funny lip, I used to call it, but if anybody made fun of her we used to beat them up. She used to make funny faces to make us laugh, she would put her tongue up through the roof of her mouth and riggle it outside her nose. She always made us cry laughing. Every time she went into hospital we all used to hope that one day she would come home beautiful.

Betty had a lot of brothers and sisters, Pendry was the oldest boy. Betty's sister Beryl was very pretty. We would watch her making up her face before she went to work in the biscuit factory. It would take about an hour. After she finished she put all the make up back into her shoe box and hid it somewhere upstairs. We would wait for her to go and then we found it under the bed. Didn't we have some fun with that shoe box.

Eileen was the oldest sister and I remember her teeth, they were like diamonds shining and she was a beautiful girl and later our Eileen as we called her went to live with her grandmother, Auntie Lil Clarke in High Street.

Eileen went to Cardiff to work and met her husband who was a foreign man. She didn't live a long life, she died very young.

Death's Door

My big sister May, was taken very ill and when Doctor Verity came he wanted to take her straight away to the hospital because she had suspected meningitis. My Mam said if she's going to die she is to die at home. During that time Mam nursed her day and night and my sister lost all her hair. Gradually she started to get better and as we lived in High Street where there were a few shops, our Mam put our May in the front window so she could see everybody shopping in the High Street.

Our May wouldn't eat nor drink and it was a very difficult time for my mother. We used to go over to the British and get the spring water out of the mountain to try and make her drink. She got better and when she got married she had five children. She craved for Mackeson Stout and when her husband was working afternoons he bought her enough stout to last the week. One night it got the better of her and she drank the lot. She had beautiful babies, they were 9lb when born. Thank the Lord our May survived to rear these children.

British Mountain opposite our village

All the people over the British used to do their shopping on a Wednesday and Friday morning, everybody was out paying their rent and the cheque man and insurance man Howell, so Mam's door was always open for a cup of tea but I think they came especially for a taste of her home made wine. The cheque man came every week for the money. Mam used to pay a few shillings a week to buy us new clothes, also a few shillings for a death insurance to bury us.

The Clarkes

My mother was a Clarke before she married my father Joseph Harris, Mam's name was Beat. Her Mam died young so Mam and her older sister Lydia had to bring that family up.

Auntie Lydia got married first but her husband wasn't very good to her, he used to hit her. One day Mam's older brother Jim tried to stop him but uncle Jim landed up with a broken nose.

One of my mother's brothers, uncle Olly Clarke married Auntie Lil and had 24 children. My mother said Auntie Lil was afraid for him to put his trousers on the bed because he was so fertile.

Carnival Day

Our Harold wanted to dress up. So we were all day cutting old rags up to make him a cowboy suit. The carnival went great and our Harold had 1st prize. He gave it to our May and when she opened it, it was a lovely silk head scarf. She put it on her head and asked Mam for a mirror to look in. We were all scared for her because she didn't know that she was bald. Our Harold started making funny faces in the mirror and we all ended up laughing.

Llanover Road - Cleaning Day

Len and I one Sunday went to see his grandfather Lewis. He wasn't in the house so we went down the garden to look for him and lo and behold there was a ladder leaning on the house and when we looked up he was putting boiling black tar on the roof. Grandpa Lewis was then 90 years of age and a very stubborn old man. Grandpa Grinnel had a Welsh corgie dog called Rex and when grandpa played the piano the dog would sing with him. They were like a double act, it was so funny to see and when grandpa played louder the dog would sing higher and louder as well. Every other week Pat, Len's sister and her Auntie Doll would walk over to Llanover Road to clean grandpa's house and one day Auntie Doll went upstairs but she came strait back down, *'Dad! What have you been doing upstairs, its in a terrible mess'*. Dust was an inch thick everywhere. He said *'I've knocked a hole in the wall and put all my money in there and papered over it'*. We always wondered whoever moved into that house after him, whatever would they find. When they dug the garden also, what would they find?

Limousine Time

It was my granddaughter Jade's 16th birthday last week, so my daughter Julie hired a Limousine for her and her friends to go to a disco down in Cardiff Bay. After they went my 13-year old granddaughter, Angharad cried her eyes out because she was too young to go. She said to her mother when I'm 13 years old in August, I want a limousine like our Jade. We don't know where she's going to go in it. MacDonalds is the only place I can think of. We'll wait and see. How things have changed since I was Queen of the Ash Tip.

My daughter spoils her girls rotten. Jade is having a party down at Cardiff Bay, a disco with eight of her friends and her Mam has ordered a Limousine like the film stars have to take them and bring them back home.

The Gronows

Where have all the years gone. The Gronows are still here but I don't hear many with a Cockney accent now, they are all Welsh to the bone now. I went to bingo at the Mecca, Cwmbran and I bumped into Ede, she married Albert Gronow when he was in Germany after the war. They came over and settled with the rest of their family. Ede said they have just had a lovely new granddaughter, a baby girl and there's still plenty of room for more. I don't think there are many Gronows in Hendon now as they are here at home with us.

We were united as families, living different worlds apart but we have all landed up as one Big Welsh Lot.

George married a Scots girl and brought her home. When we are all together singing there was a sound to be heard, with all different accents.

Television and Record Players

Leonard's dad was always one of the first to buy any new fangled gadgets. We went up on a Sunday and he had bought a record player. The records were so big that he had to buy a cabinet to put them in. You could hear it playing at the top of the street.

New invention called a television

Len's uncle Bill from Llanover Road, Blaenavon bought the first television set with a thick piece of glass in front of it to make it look bigger. We were all invited to go up and see it on Monday night. It would start about 6pm for the Evening News. We all sat around mesmerised waiting for that first picture to come on the screen, but nothing happened, only spots before our eyes. When it came to, uncle Bill hadn't put the aerial up properly so we all went home disappointed.

Things started happening fast when Mr. Loveday opened an Electric shop in High Street. He had everything in it, but the only way people could buy anything was by paying him a few shillings a week.

He had a good electrician working for him, his name was Colwyn Little. He lived next door to us. He was very clever and always messing around with wires. One day when we were playing out the back he called us kids in to see what he had made. He had all these leads on the table and they were connected up to a big light bulb and he said *'Watch now'* and when he switched on the power there was a picture on it. The first home made television ever to be seen. Mr. Little was very well liked in our community and later became our Mayor of Pontypool.

Marriage and honeymoon in London

Len and I were getting married, 14th March 1953 and we were going to London for our honeymoon. The war was over but things were still on ration so we had to take our ration books with us. Before we went, Len's father had booked everything up for us to see.

We went everywhere, the Tower of London, London Zoo, Oxford Street and we had spaghetti in a little café in Piccadilly Circus. The best of all was the show we saw on the stage, it was called The Follies Bergere. The girls were so close we could have been in the Show. They didn't have any clothes on except one girl, she had some tassels on her breasts and

The honeymoon in London.

they went round and round when the music started. Leonard was never quite same again! The Hotel was very big, it was called The Regents Palace and there were a lot of people there, especially Americans in uniform, they looked smashing.

We came down to breakfast one morning and there were a lot of girls making a fuss over a man on the next table, he had won a World Fight the night before. March 1953. There was a dance in the Hotel in the week and we decided to go. We put our best wedding gear on and when we got out of the lift everybody was dressed in evening clothes, dicky bows and tiaras, so we got a taxi and landed up in Hammersmith Palace. We had to pay half a crown to go in because there was a big band playing that night. It was wonderful.

The next morning the telephone rang in our bedroom. I was too nervous to answer it and so was Len. In the end I gave in and answered it, a voice said *'please Madam, would you pick your ration books up at the desk before you leave'*. We were having such a lovely time, we nearly forgot about them.

The main reception desk was in the main hall and I asked the clerk if I could have Mr. & Mrs. Grinnell's ration books. After a short time she came back looking

Our wedding 1953.

rather worried. *'I'm sorry Madam we can only find Leonard Grinnell's, we cannot find yours anywhere'*. I went back up in the lift to our room and I sat on the bed and said to my husband *'What are we going to do. I won't be able to have any food when we go home'* and in a split second I remembered my ration book was in my maiden name of Annie Harris, what a relief! We were going to celebrate our wedding anniversary every year in London after that, but alas it took 25 years to accomplish it again.

Electricity and lighting up time

On arrival home from honeymoon everybody in the village was having electricity put in, all except my Mam. *'No way'* she said *'it's too dangerous and when it rains we'll all be electrocuted'*. Mam let us have the front room as a bedsit to live in so we persuaded her to let us have an electric light put in that one room, she never ever turned it on. She was so afraid of it.

The honeymoon in London.

We both worked hard and luckily we managed to save enough for a deposit on two small cottages on Stanley Road. The cottages were in such a bad state no-one would buy them. We paid £250 and another £500 to have them made up. When the builders finished we could have sold them over and over again. One couple even offered us any asking price. That was nearly 50 years ago and I'm still living there today, July 2002.

Our wild scooter days

Julie was about 5 years old and she used to love for her and her friends to ride around the front lawn on her dad's Vespa Scooter. When we went to the pictures down the valley we used to put her in between us on the bike and one day as we were coming home we saw a policeman in front of us, so I put my coat right up over her head to hide her. We didn't get stopped but just imagine three pair of legs showing each side of the bike.

One day I wanted to have a go so Leonard told me what to do. We went on to our front lawn and he said *'gently let the clutch out'*, and the next thing I knew I was in the hedge, it's a good job I wasn't driving on the road. The first time Leonard went out on it he came off. Practice makes the Master so they say but Leonard still came off the bike later in an accident. One of my neighbours saw it as she was coming home on the bus. She ran straight to my house to tell me. It happened about one mile from where we lived. I just dropped everything and ran to where he was. When I got there I could see broken glass on the road, but Leonard was nowhere to be seen. I was looking for blood on the road but thank goodness there wasn't any. I shouted to the signalman, Mr. Hammonds, *'have you seen my husband who has just come off his bike'*. He replied, *'it's alright love he's gone home'*. What happened was, he had gone another way home and I missed him.

Our friends had a motorbike and sidecar. They had a little girl, a bit older than our Julie so we decided to take a trip to Porthcawl. Julie got in the sidecar with their little girl and we followed behind. She cried all the way there because she wanted to be on the scooter with us. When we arrived home that night I said *'never again'* I had a job to walk, it was too far to ride on the back of Leonard's scooter.

Leonard used to go to work on his bike every day but one week it rained so bad that he was coming home ringing wet so we decided to save for a car.

Hand me downs

My sister May was years older than me and much bigger in size but when she had anything new I always had her *'leavings off'*. I used to make them fit and I remember a coat that she had, it was fawn and brown squares with a tie belt. I was thrilled to bits the day she gave it to me. I was about 16/17 years old and I was courting Leonard Grinnell from Blaenavon at that time. That night I had a date with him at the top of the hill. I wore my new coat and I thought I was the cat's whiskers in it. I saw Len in the distance and as I got nearer I could see he didn't recognise me. Eventually he stood back and said *'What are we going to play tonight, draughts?'*. I never wore that coat again.

Courting Days

Della, my friend started to date Ken Williams one of the boys in our village and every Sunday afternoon, Len, me, Della and Ken would go up the mountain. Della and Ken under one tree and Len and I under the other. It was my birthday and Len gave me a gold necklace but I lost it, anyway when we went up the mountain the next week the necklace was there under our tree. It was as rusty as anything because it had rained all that week. I wondered if I'd ever have gold again.

Auntie Doll and Uncle Cliff's suppers

Leonard and I stated courting strong. I had promised his mother and father that I would go up to meet them both. Len met me off the bus and I was so nervous, that he had to take me back home on the bus to Garndiffaith. Later on I did pluck up the courage to meet them. He also had a sister Pat who was 10 years younger than him. It wasn't until I met them that I found out that Leonard Grinnell, my boyfriend was a fantastic piano player, so was his Dad, but not as good as Len. I started going up to his home on weekends and would sleep at his Auntie Dolls with his cousin Maureen. I'll never forget the Sunday suppers that Auntie Doll would cook. It would be a huge fry up, left overs from dinner. There was always a big chunk of fresh bread to go with it. She was a good cook and we were always very full when we left that table. Everyone in the family was there including Maureen's boyfriend Dennis Davies who was from the Garn, same as me. We both married into the family afterwards.

Len's dad was very heavy on the musical side and when he played the piano he would thump the music out. One day Leonard was going to work on the bus and sat next to one of the local boys. He said *'was you up the club last night Leonard?'* to which he replied *'No'*. *'Well there was a chap playing the piano who was bloody terrible, everybody was leaving the club and it had emptied by 10 o'clock'*. Leonard looked straight into his face and said *'that was my Dad'*.

Long Hot Summers

We used to have long hot summer days that seemed to last forever and when the men were out of work and didn't have anything to do they would all sit outside the Hanbury Hotel on a little wall and just pass the time away talking and enjoying themselves, smoking their wronk old pipes and their Woodbines and wearing those funny flat caps.

The Indian Man

The Indian man with light brown skin and a white turban would call around all the houses every year. He had a big brown suitcase and when he opened it up it was full of lovely silk scarves and mens ties and sometimes mens socks. We always bought something off him. I always wondered where he came from as I thought everybody lived the same way as we did.

Two Timing Leonard - Revenge

After a period of a few weeks of courting Leonard, I had to meet him one night outside the Pavilion Picture House after work. I wasn't very well that day as I was in terrible pain with my finger. I had what was called a phellem, it was like a boil throbbing all the time. Leonard was waiting for me when I got off the works bus and into the cinema we went. Something was wrong, Leonard never came near me, he didn't put his arm around me or give me a kiss. When we came out of the Pavilion he told me had met another girl, her name was Joan. I knew her, she was quite fat! I said to him *'why didn't you tell me before we went into the cinema?'*. I felt really awful, I didn't know whether to cry for my finger or him. As we were walking up the road, I saw a red Western Welsh bus coming so I just ran and got on it, leaving him in the middle of the road. Love hurts - that was my first encounter. After that I went back on the Sunday Monkey Parade with Betty up Cwmavon Road. We were with a gang of boys from Blaenavon and who should be walking past us was Leonard and his best friend Ron who was evacuated here from Dover. He looked at me and smiled but I turned my head away. I hadn't forgot the hurt he caused me.

Monday, next Day

I came home from work as usual and Mam said *'There's a letter there for you'*. (I could see it had been steamed open and closed back up). When I read it, he was sorry and wanted to go back with me so I wrote back to this letter saying *'You've got a cheek, wait until I see you FACE TO FACE'*.

Wednesday night came around and off I went to our Varteg Dance Hall. I was dancing around with one of the boys and there was an *'Excuse me'* and suddenly there was a tap on his shoulder, it was Leonard, he said *'Here I am FACE TO FACE'*. Cheeky as anything, after which he walked me home and we started seeing each other once more. He had me wrapped around his little finger.

A few weeks later it started to snow heavy on the Wednesday dance night so the bus never turned up from Blaenavon, the snow was too deep. Only local boys were there to dance with, it was a very quiet night. When the dance finished one of the local boys that I knew very well, started to walk with me through the snow because we lived the same way. We were laughing and talking when he said to me *'there's a girl I'm crazy about but I don't know how to tell her'*. I said *'If you don't tell her how is she going to find out'*. With that, he swung me around and kissed me. He knocked me off my feet, it was devine. I promised to meet him at the Park Cinema few days later, so when I got home that night I wrote a letter to Leonard Grinnell and told him I didn't love him anymore and I also told him a big fib. I said I wanted time to think and I was going to go out with my girl friends again. I left the letter with my Mam to give him as he was coming down that day. Mam didn't know I was finishing with him. Anyway off I went to meet Roy, that was his name, he was 6ft tall and very good looking. We went to see Doris Day in the film *Its Magic*. I had already seen it in the week with Leonard, so I thought if he comes looking for me he won't find me there.

When he opened the letter my Mam said *'What's the matter son?'* and he gave it to her to read. *'You go straight down to Pontypool, that's where the madam has gone'* she said. So he got on a bus to find me. First place he looked was the Pavilion cinema and he had the girl with the torch go in between every isle and seat to see if I was there, upstairs and downstairs. No luck, so he went to the next cinema the Royal and did the same thing. He came out of there making his way to the Park cinema and unluckily for us we came out at the wrong time because as we passed the corner we came smack on, FACE TO FACE. He just grabbed me and pulled me into a doorway saying *'I'm the chap that you are courting'*. He was so upset, crying his eyes out, so I left Roy and walked hand in hand with Len until we got to our house. Mam was waiting for me ready to hit me but Leonard stopped her saying *'She's been with me all night'*, he never told her I was with Roy. After that we started courting strong again and we eventually got engaged to each other and married in 1953. So you see I had my revenge at times but we were married for 42 years, very happily, until Leonard died in 1995. Mam always used to say WHO'S FOR YOU YOU'LL HAVE.

Furniture Shop

Glyn Davies decided to open a second-hand furniture shop. It went very well and soon he was buying second-hand cars and then new ones. He moved down the valley to better things because later they built a new town, called Cwmbran and a lot of our village people moved down there too and never came back.

Toy Factory and Crisp Factory

The empty building over by the Garn Garage was being looked at by some very important people. I wonder what's going on? Later they made it into a toy factory and we would climb on some boxes and look in through the window to see all those wonderful toys being made, especially the Teddy Bears. I said to Della *'I'm going to work there some day'* and years later I did.

I was the machinist for the Marks and Spencer Teddy Bears. I used to sew 7 dozen a day for £1 day. No wonder my back is so bad.

Women started to earn money and after the toy factory left to go to New Inn, Pontypool to a bigger factory, a crisp factory opened and put work on the Garn for a lot of women but I didn't fancy that, it was like a fish shop and you would smell of salt and vinegar. The women who worked there loved it because they had a bit of independence.

Staff and teddy bears at the Chiltern toy factory.

Pigeon Club

The Pigeon Club was under the Hanbury Hotel, Garndiffaith and some of the men would pass their time away looking after their pigeons. They were very pretty colours but mostly grey and they would race them. Melvin Watkins loved his birds but they used to make an awful lot of mess on people's roofs but no-one ever complained. It was part of the village life and we all had cats and dogs (you could always find a home for the kittens and pups without any trouble) or an animal of some kind. It was a joy to watch those birds fly all around Garndiffaith, Varteg and Talywain but they always came straight home to their roosts. The men would go far and wide looking for new breeds.

Famous Film Stars

We all started to go dancing regularly up the Mostyn Hall but we always walked there which was about 3 miles and walked back after the dance was over. One night we filled the road all holding hands and a big van stopped right on the top of the mountain and offered us a lift home. When we got in the van it was full of big flat tins containing the week's films for our local cinema. The driver would deliver for miles around. To think I was riding with all those film stars. He picked us up every week afterwards. We didn't know his name but I will never forget that lift with the film man. When it was very dark we had to follow these big stones that were on the side of the mountain road. They were painted white and shone up in the moonlight. There were no lights on the road in those days. In later years they put cats eyes down which made it a lot better.

Foxgloves

In summer we would go and pick foxgloves off the mountain and take them into the local cemetery on top of the mountain to put on the graves. We had to pull them out of the ground because we couldn't break the stems they were so strong. When I got older I learned they were a poisonous plant but they never hurt us.

Pearls

I cannot remember exactly how I came across this one row of lovely pearls. They were in my cabinet for years. I couldn't wear them because they needed to be restrung. I was always buying bits and pieces in boot sales but I remember one of my old age pensioners giving me a row of pearls because I took her home a few times after doing her hair as she was getting frail. We were cleaning everything out and my daughter fancied the diamanté clasp on the back of the pearls and she said *'can I have these pearls Mam?'*. I said *'Yes, but you'll have to have them restrung'*.

Julie took the pearls to a jeweller in Cardiff and he said it would cost £25 to have them restrung. *'Why is it that much?'* Julie asked. He said *'My dear, these pearls are better quality than I have in the window, they are worth over £1000'*. What a lovely surprise.

Granddad's Wine Glass

Leonard's grandfather Grinnell had died and they had to clear the house which was left to Len's Dad, after which they all moved to High Street in Blaenavon. Apparently Grandpa Grinnell had a brother in the Navy many moons ago and there was a brass rum glass he had brought home. I have this rum glass to this day and it came off Nelson's ship. I'd love to check up and find out if it is real, there is a number on the bottom, a number 2. We never drink out of it but it's been on my shelf for over 40 years. Who knows we could be worth thousands and not know it? After my days I hope somebody will have it checked by an antique dealer, but DON'T THROW IT OUT.

Staffordshire Blacksmith

My mother left me a Staffordshire China Blacksmith which I have treasured all my life. He is high up in the corner of my living room and has been looking down on us for years. I bet he could tell us some stories. He is absolutely gorgeous, I wouldn't sell him for anything, he's priceless.

Hospital Hairdresser - 1969

I was the hospital hairdresser for eight hospitals and sometimes I had more trouble with the cleaners on the wards than any of the patients. One cleaner in the Royal Gwent used to pick on me as soon as I came into the ward. She would say *'you left hair in the sink'* I never did, or *'your drier makes marks all over my floor'* anything to upset me. One day I was very busy so I set off earlier in the morning than usual. My first hospital was Panteg maternity. I got everything out of my car to go into the first ward and the Sister came out and said *'you cannot come in yet its too early'*, so I put everything back into the car and went on my way. Guess what happened next, I had a puncture in my car. I thought this is just not my day. Eventually I got to the Royal Gwent and as I made my way into the ward I could see the cleaner coming towards me. Before she could say anything I stopped dead and shouted at her *'DON'T YOU START ON ME TODAY, I AM IN THE RIGHT MOOD FOR YOU'*. She was so shocked she said to me *'do you want a cup of tea luv?'*. After that she never complained to me again, so it pays sometimes to OPEN YOUR MOUTH, DOESN'T IT? We became good pals after that.

Julie's First Cut

When I opened the Hair Salon in 1970 at Talywain my daughter was 13 years old and her hair was blond and long right down her back. *'Mam'* she said *'you are cutting all my friends hair in the 'bubble and feather' cut'*, that was a short cut. *'Why can't I have mine done?'* I didn't want to cut it and her father said *'NO'* but she kept on and on until one day I gave her the money and said *'I'm not doing it, go down to Pontypool and have it done'*. She said *'I want you to do do it'* and she wouldn't go, so eventually I gave in. I still have her lovely locks in a plastic bag. Gone was that baby look and now it was growing-up time and she started to come to the Salon after school to sweep up and make the tea. As time went by she decided she wanted to be a Hairdresser, so when she left school I took her on as an apprentice. The weeks went by and it was time for her to do some cutting. I arranged for some young girls to come in as guinea pigs and have their hair done free. Julie was OK until the moment I put the scissors in her hand and then she panicked, dropped the scissors and went rushing out of the salon door and ran home to her father.

We had some lovely old pensioners, Mr. & Mrs. Richards who lived near the shop and they were very fond of Julie and they had watched her grow up from a baby. Mr. Richards volunteered to be a guinea pig for her so she agreed to cut Mr. Richard's hair and then she did it a few times

My brother Will's wedding to Rene and as I am the flower girl on the left the difference in age between myself and my brother is quite apparent. Stood next to my sister-in-law is Mr. Hudson who owned the local fish and chip shop before my brother and his wife took it over.

after that. One day he came in and sat in the chair and I left Julie on her own to do his hair. All of a sudden there was a scream, Julie had cut Mr. Richards ear lobe and the blood was everywhere. We stopped the bleeding and put a plaster on it, but it didn't stop Mr. Richards, he came back for more and never left us. What a lovely gentleman he was. Julie carried on and has been hairdressing now for 30 years. She has her own business in Cardiff and is doing very well.

Twenty-five Pence Antique Brooch

My daughter and I loved looking around boot sales on a Sunday morning and we did one ourselves sometimes. We used to love it. One day I picked up this pretty little brooch, it was only small and I said to Julie *'do you want it?'* she said *'no thanks, I don't like brooches'*. I bought

Len's retirement from Glascoed Works in 1980. He started there in 1959 but had to take an early retirement because of ill health when he was just 50 years of age. He had many workmates while working there and was particularly 'pally' with Gary Lane from Blaenavon, a good friend for over 30 years.

it and left it in the cupboard for about 6 months because I had started to get trouble with my fingers, arthritis the Doctor had said. Unfortunately I couldn't get my eternity ring and a few others on. It was our 25th Wedding Anniversary and we decided to go to London on our second honeymoon. Before we went we decided to go to Abergavenny Market on the Tuesday. Len said *'why don't you sell some of your rings, it will pay for our weekend in London?'*. Our Julie didn't want them, so I said OK. That morning I was getting ready to go and I pinned the 25p brooch in my jumper and off we went.

The first buyer we saw only offered me £8 for my eternity ring. I was disgusted at that price because it was beautiful and as we walked away he said *'I'll give you £125 for that brooch in your jumper'*. I was shocked because I didn't realise it was real. I said *'No thank you'* to the dealer, I thought he's a cheat! I bet it's worth more than that. My husband wanted me to sell it to him and have the money for our London weekend. Anyway I took it to another dealer in the Market and he examined it through his little magnifying glass and said there were 60 baby pearls set in green enamel and he thought it was Victorian. He said he could probably get £250 for it and he would sell it for us to a bigger dealer. I said *'No thank you it's worth more than that'*. My husband went mad with me, I can be awfully stubborn sometimes. The following week I went to Cardiff shopping and I called in Phillips the Auctioneers and left the brooch with them. I had to wait a long time for the next auction but I didn't mind. Then a letter and cheque came through the post. I was so excited opening it, the brooch had sold for £350. I had to pay them £51 for selling it for me but look at the profit I made out of a 25p brooch - £299. How's that for making money. My husband just laughed and said *'Find some more'*.

Biking Days to Blaenavon

During the time Leonard was in the army I decided to buy a bike and I used to go and see his Mam, Dad and sister Pat. It was hard work biking up but it was lovely coming back. I didn't have any lights on my bike so I would leave Blaenavon before it got dark. One night I was a bit late and as I was nearing the Varteg I could see Bobby Clarke our local policeman coming towards me. I got off the bike and started to walk but he was very nice to me and gave me a warning not to ride my bike in the dark without lights. Later on I fell off my bike at Talywain and when Leonard came home I had two black eyes and bruises. I looked a proper mess with all the swellings as well. But he still loved me, but I never rode that bike again.

How did my school friends get on in life

Betty got married twice and had a little girl by her first husband. Her family has grown and she has three great grandchildren and they are all blond like Betty.

Della was married twice and she had six children and when they grew up she went to college and passed her City and Guilds. She now makes fantastic Wedding and Birthday cakes and she is now a teacher herself. Who would have thought I would be a business woman! So my advice to anyone is *'THERE IS NO SUCH THING AS CAN'T DO IT'.*

A view of Garndiffaith as it looked in the 1970s.

Epitaph

Sadly Annie died in January 2004 never seeing her book being published. However her family and friends know full well that she would have been so proud of this finished article and that they would enjoy reading her work.